ENCOUNTERS WITH MATERIALS IN EARLY CHILDHOOD EDUCATION

Encounters With Materials in Early Childhood Education rearticulates understandings of materials—blocks of clay, sheets of paper, brushes, and paints—to formulate what happens when we think with materials and apply them to early childhood development and classrooms. The book develops ways of thinking about materials that are more sustainable and insightful than what most children in the Western world experience today through capitalist narratives.

Through a series of ethnographic events and engagement with existing ideas of relationality in the visual arts, feminist ethics, science studies, philosophy, and anthropology, *Encounters With Materials in Early Childhood Education* highlights how materials can be conceptualized as active participants in early childhood education and as generators of human insight. A variety of examples show how educators, young children, and researchers have engaged in thinking with materials in early years classrooms and explore what materials are capable of in their encounters with other materials and with children.

Please visit the companion website at www.encounterswithmaterials.com for additional features, including interviews with the authors and the teachers featured in the book, videos and photographs of the classroom narratives described in these pages, and an ongoing blog of the authors' ethnographic notes.

Veronica Pacini-Ketchabaw is Professor of Early Childhood Education in the Faculty of Education at Western University, Canada.

Sylvia Kind is Faculty Instructor, Department of Early Childhood Care and Education at Capilano University, Canada, and Adjunct Assistant Professor, Faculty of Graduate Studies at the University of Victoria, Canada.

Laurie L. M. Kocher is Faculty Instructor, Department of Early Childhood Care and Education at Capilano University, Canada.

ENCOUNTERS WITH MATERIALS IN EARLY CHILDHOOD EDUCATION

Veronica Pacini-Ketchabaw,
Sylvia Kind, and Laurie L. M. Kocher

Routledge
Taylor & Francis Group

NEW YORK AND LONDON

First published 2017
by Routledge
711 Third Avenue, New York, NY 10017

and by Routledge
2 Park Square, Milton Park, Abingdon, Oxon OX14 4RN

Routledge is an imprint of the Taylor & Francis Group, an informa business

Library of Congress Cataloging-in-Publication Data
Names:Pacini-Ketchabaw,Veronica. | Kind,Silvia. | Kocher,Laurie L. M.,1959–
Title: Encounters with materials in early childhood education / Veronica
    Pacini-Ketchabaw, Sylvia Kind, and Laurie L. M. Kocher.
Description: New York : Routledge, 2017. | Includes bibliographical
    references and index.
Identifiers: LCCN 2016014478 | ISBN 9781138821453 (hardback) |
    ISBN 9781138821460 (pbk.) | ISBN 9781315743257 (ebook)
Subjects: LCSH: Early childhood education—Activity programs. |
    Teaching—Aids and devices.
Classification: LCC LB1139.35.A37 P33 2017 | DDC 372.21—dc23
LC record available at https://lccn.loc.gov/2016014478

ISBN: 978-1-138-82145-3 (hbk)
ISBN: 978-1-138-82146-0 (pbk)
ISBN: 978-1-315-74325-7 (ebk)

Typeset in Bembo
by Apex CoVantage, LLC

This book is dedicated to the children and educators who have been our inspiration and our companions in the process of experimenting with materials.

CONTENTS

FIGURES

ACKNOWLEDGMENTS

We are very grateful to the children, educators, and families who have so enthusiastically participated in this work and continue to provide inspiration. We have learned so much as we discover new possibilities together, and we are changed. We dedicate this book to them.

We thank our editor, Leslie Prpich of Beyond Words, for her capable editorial and writing support. Her careful attention and caring engagement with the material she encountered enlivened our manuscript. We cannot imagine working without her—she is beyond amazing.

We also thank the Social Sciences and Humanities Research Council of Canada for generously supporting our research.

1

THINKING WITH MATERIALS

In the early childhood classroom, educators and children gather around materials to investigate, negotiate, converse, and share. A block of clay, a brush, pots of paint, a brilliant sheet of paper, a heavy rectangular wooden block, a thin piece of willow charcoal—materials beckon and pull us in. They live, speak, gesture, and call to us. Materials can evoke memories, narrate stories, invite actions, and communicate ideas.

This book sets out to experiment with pedagogies of relationality that emerge when we encounter materials as active participants in early childhood education. Nothing in its pages acts as an appropriate model of practice. There is nothing to rehearse, nothing to appropriate. The book is about *encounters*. Encounters that are not necessarily good or bad. These are risky, worldly encounters that affect us, provoke us to think and feel, attach us to the world and detach us from it, force us into action, demand from us, prompt us to care, concern us, bring us into question.

Experimenting with these encounters entails nudging ourselves to experience them differently. We do not find, nor are we looking for, the meaning of these encounters. We are not concerned with their facts. We engage with each encounter as an event that demands its own questions, its own concerns, its own ethos. We inhabit each encounter. We are situated in each encounter's situatedness.

Eventful Material Relations

Encounters With Materials in Early Childhood Education aims to tell stories of what happens when we think *with* materials, when we choose to see materials as movements, as encounters, as assemblages, as ecologies, as time. Materials live in the world in multiple ways (Bennett, 2004). In the chapters that follow, we think with five materials that are often found in early childhood spaces: paper, charcoal, paint, clay, and blocks. We treat these materials as active and participatory. They set things in motion, incite questions, produce ideas. In other words, they become productive moments.

Throughout the book, materials generate insights by provoking human and nonhuman others. We pay attention to a wide spectrum of forces and movements: how materials move through time and space; how materials move us, physically and emotionally; how time moves; how air moves; how bodies move; and more.

Thinking *with* materials transforms early childhood education, provoking educators to notice how materials and young children live entangled lives in classrooms, how they change each other through their mutual encounters. We are curious about the ways such a shift in perspective might change our interactions with materials, children, other educators—and perhaps even change the nature of our engagement with society and the world.

The greater goal of this book is to reassemble early childhood spaces as vibrant social-ecological-material-affective-discursive ecologies in which humans and nonhumans are always in relation. Relationality, therefore, is central to *Encounters With Materials*.

In this chapter, we tell stories of how materials are conceptualized in early childhood education and how we think of materials throughout this book. We outline the project this book is based on: what we did, the questions we asked, how we integrated materials through the arts, how we used video and photography. In other words, this chapter is where our theoretical and methodological frameworks are set into motion. Yet, this introduction is not written to support the book's structure. Like the book itself, it is written through diffractive movements to produce new possibilities.

Materials in Early Childhood

Engagements with materials are certainly not new in the early childhood literature. Since the 19th century, early childhood scholars have emphasized materials' importance for the development and education of young children. Frederick Froebel's gifts, the first educational toys developed in the 1800s, have marked materials' central role in early education (Prochner, 2011), but John Dewey (1897) reminded us more than a century ago that "the child's own instincts and powers furnish the material and give the starting point for all education" (art. 1, para. 3).

Today, scholars continue to highlight the importance of materials in young children's learning. Processes such as painting with a brush and working with clay are seen as activities that contribute to children's social, physical, emotional, and creative development (Golomb, 1992; Lowenfeld & Brittain, 1987; Matthews,

2003). The majority of texts available emphasize what to do with materials, yet say little about how one might think *with* them.

While movements have been made toward thinking of children's artistic explorations of materials as languages (Pelo, 2007), even early childhood centers that integrate the arts in their practices typically use developmental understandings of materials and artistic processes. There may be an interest and desire to engage with the arts as a visual language, yet without a depth of conceptual understanding, too often children's art is viewed as literal representations of self, experience, or knowledge. Materials are described as "bones" of curriculum (Carter & Curtis, 2007) in a developmental progression from exploration to representation. Often, instructions on how to organize and arrange materials are first provided so that children will learn the materials' properties and functions. Then, as they become more familiar with the materials, children are encouraged to use them to represent ideas and objects.

Pedagogues in the Reggio Emilia infant and preschool programs in northern Italy have paid close attention to materials, and philosophically complex ideas have been generated from their investigations of materiality (Ceppi & Zini, 2008; Friends of Reggio, 2004; Vecchi, 2010; Vecchi & Giudici, 2004). We see today a myriad of early childhood classrooms inspired by the practices in Reggio Emilia around materials (Callaghan, 2002; Fraser, 2006; Gerst, 1998, 2002, 2003; Kocher, 1999, 2004, 2009, 2010; MacDonald-Carlson, 1997, 2003; Rosen, 2009; Tarr, 2005; Tarr, Bjartveit, Kostiuk, & McCowan, 2009; Wien, 2008; Wong, 2006; Young, 2001).

We, too, have been greatly inspired by the Reggio Emilia pedagogical work. Despite the work's significance for our field's development, though, little of the Reggio-inspired early childhood literature focuses on how materials can take part in shaping ideas. This is the focus of our book.

The connections that *Encounters With Materials in Early Childhood Education* creates might surprise some readers. Instead of suggesting that carefully selected, beautifully organized materials be offered to children to experiment with and to represent their ideas and theories, this book thinks *with* materials—alongside them, listening to and caring for them, being with and being for things, exploring an ecology and ethics of things (Benso, 2000). We engage in thinking beyond instrumentalism, which reduces things to surface qualities and functions and treats materials as merely what mediates learning and developmental processes (e.g., Rule & Stewart, 2002; Trimis & Savva, 2009).

We investigate how materials "speak back" to children in agentic ways, extending and broadening the important body of knowledge on Reggio Emilia–inspired practices. Simultaneously, we generate original research to inform what Hillevi Lenz Taguchi (2010) refers to as an *intra-active pedagogy* that shifts attention from intra- and interpersonal relationships toward a material–discursive relationship among all living organisms and the material environment, such as objects and artifacts, spaces and places.

Encounters With Materials in Early Childhood Education challenges understandings of materials that define them from a scientific, rational, or functional viewpoint and through predictable properties of color, shape, density, mass, friction, and gravity. We contest deeply rooted cultural dichotomies—animate versus inanimate, active versus passive, and self versus other, to name a few (Bennett, 2010)—that lead us, often unconsciously, to think of ourselves as animate agents who act on passive, inanimate materials. We ask: What if humans' role in shaping materials is not as central as we believe? What if materials shape us as much as we shape them? What if we pay attention to the effects of things and to how things move together, not asking what an object or a thing or a material *is,* but what does a material *do?*

In this book, materials themselves propose particular possibilities. Materials do not just feel or act differently from each other, or have different properties, or produce different forms and images. They also provoke different ways of thinking as a child engages and works with them.

A block, for instance, is not just a tool for building. A block evokes particular ways of thinking, processing ideas, and making meaning that are profoundly different from the ways one works with paint, charcoal, paper, or clay, for example. In drawing a human figure or in using a camera to create a particular image of a person, the subject may be the same, yet engaging with different media and processes results in different perceptions and ways of thinking through the subject.

This means that how we think about materials shapes what is possible to do with them. For example, if we think of clay as a sculptural material used for making objects, that thought suggests certain engagements. We may set out individual slabs or balls of clay on a table and give directions or support in how to create particular objects. We may talk about form, texture, structure, and balance. We may subtly or directly encourage individual sculptural objects.

What we think clay is for shapes our experience with it, and the language we use to talk about the experience constructs particular meanings. If, on the other hand, we think about movement, place, impermanence, and relationality, then we may consider the possibility of moving toward and away from the clay, attending to the relationship of clay to its surroundings, and inviting interaction with others.

These concepts give structure to and shape the investigations with the material. And so we may set the clay out in other ways, for instance, as a big block in the center of a large mat on the floor, as several blocks stacked so they echo a child's height, in a space with several overhead projectors to facilitate a complex play of shadow, bodies, and movement. These various ways of setting out the clay do not just invite different interactions. They also shape what and how we see and the meanings we construct of the experience.

The "Material Encounters in Early Childhood Education" Project

This book works with pedagogical events collected through the "Material Encounters in Early Childhood Education" project, a visual ethnographic study conducted in two early childhood centers in Canada and supported by the Social Sciences and Humanities Research Council. The project's main goal has been to engage in an art-based collaborative inquiry to experiment with the complexities and possibilities of engaging with materials' relationality in early childhood spaces.

Inquiring Into Materiality

Over a period of three years, children, educators, and researchers became interested in what might happen to pedagogies when their focus is not solely on how children think about materials, or how materials should be presented to children, or what children's or educators' intentions are in relation to materials. Our focus became paying careful attention to materials in interaction. Through that process, we discovered that materials have a life of their own in classrooms and that these lives matter immensely for how we think and act in classrooms. We took materials seriously, not to romanticize them or to think of them as humans, but to attend to what they do when they participate in classrooms. We encountered each material as already filled with histories and stories, and also as an event that would allow us to ask questions and provoke inquiries.

In our weekly inquiries with children and educators, we asked: What does it mean to think *with* things? How does each material evoke particular invitations and provocations? How does each material live differently among/with/between other things and among/with/between young children? How are materials implicated in a classroom's movements? These questions framed our collaborations.

Experimentation

Materials, objects, places, and environments are inextricably bound to experimentation; thus, experimentation was key to our inquiries. The work of philosophers Gilles Deleuze and Félix Guattari (1987) helped us to conceptualize our experimentations with materials. Experimentation is a complex social-affective-political phenomenon that actively extends experience (Guattari, 1995). It opens up worlds and creates new venues for thinking and doing (Stengers, 2005). It reveals what human and nonhuman bodies can do and produce when they encounter each other. We embraced experimentation in our collaboration to transform life in the early childhood centers.

We committed ourselves to see encounters among materials, objects, places, and humans as part of the flow of experience. We created pedagogies that assume that we are never separate from the world, that we are made up of relations. Following Deleuze and Guattari, we conceptualized thought as experimentation: Thought creates itself through encounters. We experimented with the ideas that stories are told, forces are harnessed, and roles are performed through thought.

Through experimentation we discovered how something works by relations among the parts of assemblages, structures, flows, and connections. In this way we assumed teaching and learning as processes of creating what Deleuze and Guattari (1987) called lines of flight. By testing new and unpredictable mixes of bodies, forces, and things, we invented. Our process of inquiry into the unknown became embedded in the experimentation of experience, with all its unpredictable connections. Our experiments were not without risk, of course. Outcomes could never be predicted or known in advance. There was always the danger of reproducing the same, of decomposing one or more elements of an assemblage too quickly. Certainly, our project has been imperfect. It has been marked by struggle and, at times, resistance. The work has been slow, often challenging and unsettling. Yet, we committed to staying with the trouble, as Haraway (2008) suggests, that our experimentations brought to us.

Experimentation brought life to our sedimented early childhood discourses, increased our capacity to act in the world, and produced new forms of living (see O'Sullivan, 2006). It allowed us to open up perceptions and understandings of what is possible in the classroom. We engaged with children, materials, narratives, and each other as if they act on us and we act on them, entering into complex, entangled networks and assemblages—or, to use Lenz Taguchi's (2010) term, into intra-activity. We got to know the power, vibrancy, timeliness, possibilities, and consequences of a material.

This did not mean that we ignored children in our inquiries. We were interested in what children select, what they choose as desirable, and what they bring into their play. But we were also aware that experimentation does not only involve children's creative inventions. We worked within the tensions and ethics of listening to children's own concerns as we took seriously the materials and discourses children play with. We began from this question: How do children take the substance of their lives—the circulating images, narratives, and ideas—and make something of them, inventing, reproducing, transforming?

In the chapters that follow, we hope it becomes clearer how experimentation was encouraged in the early childhood centers, how the educators looked for ways to provoke and facilitate experimentation, how "problems" were worked with and not "managed," how most of the work that took place in the classrooms was collective and not "owned" by particular children. Through pedagogical experimentation, we aimed to create a collective context so that it was never about what individual children did, rather how we could invent together.

The Arts as Mode of Inquiry

Our collective experimentations with materials emerged through our interest in the arts. In the "Material Encounters in Early Childhood Education" project, the arts were not superfluous additions, teacher-directed activities, or even idealized examples of children's inner worlds or creativity. Instead, they were seen as integral aspects of children's daily inquiries, explorations, and learning. Art was a puzzle, a question, an encounter. As Claire Colebrook (2002) reminds us, like inquiry and research,

> art is not about knowledge, conveying "meanings" or providing information. Art is not just an ornament or style used to make data more palatable or consumable. Art may well have meanings or messages, but what makes it art is not its content but its *affect*, the sensible force or style through which it produces content.
>
> *(pp. 24–25, emphasis in original)*

Part of what art does is ask us to attend to things. It draws our attention, often to new things, or to older things said or presented in new ways. Basically, art asks us to make sense of things, or to figure them out.

As we mentioned earlier, integrating the arts into our project was not always easy. It is a commonly held misconception that art should be easy—that an artwork emerges effortlessly in a singular moment of inspiration, or that an artist knows the work in advance and an idea comes into his or her mind fully formed. There is often a large difference between an artist's idea and the realization of that idea in paint, charcoal, or clay. The process of working through an idea is not straightforward, as if the materials merely illustrate a mental image; rather, there is a dynamic interaction of thought and image, and both are shaped in the process of creating. Shaun McNiff (2008), for example, writes:

> Artistic inquiry, whether it is within the context of research or an individual person's creative expression, typically starts with the realization that you cannot define the final outcome when you are planning to do the work. . . . In the creative process, the most meaningful insights often come by surprise, unexpectedly, and even against the will of the creator.
>
> *(p. 40)*

Art also relies on failures, mistakes, and disjunctures (Kind, 2007). As Alain Toumayayan (2004) describes, artistic inspiration is a "consequence of failure . . . an accomplishment which exceeds one's powers of conception, planning and execution" (p. 93). Thus, to create is to step into the unknown with improvisation at the heart of the endeavor. Failure, struggle, uncertainty, and not knowing the outcomes in advance were at times difficult concepts for educators to embrace, yet these are essential elements of artistic practice.

Drawing on the work of Guattari (1995) and Bennett (2010), Springgay and Rotas (2014) write about classroom art as more than giving children an opportunity to explore or to have a sensory experience:

> In thinking a classroom as art, Guattari (1995) is not referring to institutionalized art but to the ethico-aesthetic paradigm, where mutant compositions will "not simply attempt to preserve the endangered species of cultural life but equally to engender conditions for the creation and development of unprecedented formations of subjectivity that have never been seen and never felt" (p. 91). Disrupting reductive practices that enforce specific ways of doing curriculum (i.e., laws and codes), the classroom as art, as an ecology—an ethico-political enunciation—"is an activity of unframing" (p. 131); a way of living differently both in schools/life, but also differently living research, vital research "which refuses to dissolve completely into the milieu of human knowledge" (Bennett, 2010, p. 3).
>
> *(Springgay & Rotas, 2014, p. 563)*

When art is understood materially, as an affective event, it becomes irreducible to function, form, and technique. In our project, it became a force of relations that made learning felt and inarticulable—in excess of language. As Springgay and Rotas put it, art became a social practice. Children were creating and were invited into thought.

The Studio

The art studio was an important element in our experimentations. The studio itself emerged and shifted through and with the project. It took many different forms and was created differently in each early childhood center at different times. In one center, we claimed a small area of a resource room that was connected to the early childhood education students' classroom, and it became a dedicated studio space. In another center, we transformed the atrium into a studio. The forest became an art studio, as did a river. Yet, we never fully defined what the studio was supposed to be. We stayed close to the idea of "not yet." We wanted to follow the rhythms and movements of the studio and wonder, What is the studio? rather than know in advance what it was or should be. Each studio evolved slowly.

In the studio, we questioned rather than accepted what things were. We asked, "What is (a) painting?" rather than trying to facilitate or plan painting projects. We held back for a while on an emphasis on what the marks and imagery represented, and attended instead to how our understanding and perception of the processes could be enlarged and altered. We wondered: When does a painting begin? When does it end? What are the rituals, rhythms, and tempo of painting?

And we experimented, sometimes rather wildly, with materials. We spent months in intense experimentation with charcoal, encounters that connected rooms, teachers, and children across the center and left resonances and traces throughout the space. And there were many other experiments as we explored, for instance, the intersections of body, dance, and painting, stretching the possibilities and feeling a sense of the lived/living relationships of body-material-surface-and-space. We watched how paint, fingers, and brush transformed the paper, or how the paint moved from easel to window, or how the light played with the paint, trees, and plexiglass painting surface when we painted.

We paid attention to how clay, when rolled into a ball, seemed to want to move along the floor or be carried around in buckets. We watched the choreography of bodies, paintbrushes, and containers of paint moving in and out and around surfaces. We attended to rituals of painting and washing, covering and recovering. We noticed and responded to how the paint colors or the clay echoed with the trees, sky, weather, and earth. And of course, as we paid attention to these things, we began to shift how we thought about, talked about, valued, and responded to children, the materials, and artistic processes.

The studio invited us to slow down, to listen to the intricate visual and sensorial details, to attend to the particularity or the "thingness" of things, and to treat things tenderly and gently. The studio was a quiet place where children could pause with us to notice the materials' movements and invitations, to follow the sounds of their drawings, to negotiate ideas, to follow lines of thought, to be with, or dwell with, ideas, processes, and materials. We hoped to develop a more textured and descriptive artistic language and a space where we could work well with delicate and fragile materials in addition to strong and robust ones so that our movements and encounters with materials, spaces, surfaces, and processes could be multifaceted, complex, and full of life.

The indoor studios at first were quite empty: one glass brick wall; a clock (which has since been put away); one or two low tables; small chairs; a selection of pods, seeds, sticks, barks, and branches; rolls of paper; and various drawing media. The studio was not a rigid place, a container for creative acts and materials, but an emergent space itself inherently creative and creating. We were not interested in filling the room, preparing it, or creating a specified "art space." We wanted to see how the studio would take shape in its use.

The studio became a place to dwell. Tim Ingold (2011), borrowing from both Heidegger and Marx, frames the difference between building and dwelling. Builders use plans, drawings, and a framework for what they are about to build, so a built form is the outcome of a prior design. Dwelling, by contrast, Ingold writes, "is intransitive: it is about the way inhabitants, singly and together, produce their own lives, and like life, it carries on" (p. 10). Dwelling, then, is not just about occupying structures. It is about being immersed in the currents of the lifeworld. Humans, of course, do build things. But the idea of dwelling takes into account processes of working with materials and not just doing something to them, and of being part of the emergent processes of bringing something into being.

We settled into an easy rhythm in the studio. At times it was a lively space, full of activity, and at times it appeared still, with just the materials. Yet even in the room's "emptiness" things were always moving: the drawings on the wall, hanging sculptures of leaves and twigs, the diffused sunlight coming through the glass bricks changing with the time of day and the weather. The seedpods and leaves moved slowly and almost imperceptibly, but were still in processes of decay, drying, curling, occasionally picking up the faint breeze from the circulation of air in the room. Ingold (2011), discussing Merleau-Ponty's concept of perception and the sentient world, writes:

> To be sentient . . . is to open up to a world, to yield to its embrace, and to resonate in one's inner being to its illuminations and reverberations . . . the sentient body, at once both perceiver and producer, traces the paths of the world's becoming in the very course of contributing to its renewal.
>
> *(p. 12)*

The room itself invited us to open up to a world of beauty, artistry, and wonder.

When in the studio, we became much more attentive and deliberate in our attention. The studio took on a new intensity as we looked at the intra-activity of materials, children, spaces, places, and bodies. We became curious about how materials move within and between the studio and the rooms in the center, and we have experimented, invented, played with, and taken time to dwell with materials like paper.

We still do not know what the studio is. It is an idea. It takes shape, sometimes temporarily outside in the field or in the forest, and it is characterized by forces and energies rather than places, rooms, and walls. We know we needed the room or the space to remind us, and others, that the work existed. The space also allowed for pauses and times of dwelling with ideas. But the studio itself, the room or the space, was only part of the project. Over time it became more like a verb, an action and acting, a function and collection of rhythms of movements. It took shape, moving, changing, becoming when we gathered to listen, watch, question, respond, invent, and experiment. It held a great sense of anticipation.

Our experimentations in the studios have been somewhat risky and often messy encounters, yet ones full of joy and adventure. The traces of these explorations still resonate and are felt in the studios.

Encounters With Materials *and the Reggio Emilia Project*

This book would be incomplete if we did not include further commentary on the connections between our project and the artistic project of the Reggio Emilia infant and preschool programs (http://www.reggiochildren.it/?lang=en). We are indebted to their important work. Yet, we do not conceptualize our work as following a Reggio Emilia approach to early childhood.

Jonah Lehrer (2012), in his book *Imagine*, discusses Bob Dylan's process of composing. He describes how Dylan understands his creative process as one of love and theft, and how it begins when he finds a sound or song that "touches the bone" (p. 246). Through close study he then tries to deconstruct the sound to figure out how it works. In the same way, the studio work in Reggio Emilia has "touched the bone" of countless early childhood educators. So many of us have been inspired by how the Reggio educators have embraced the arts as central to children's learning processes. They have engaged with the arts, not as an add-on or extra, a subject of study, or even a brief experiment, but as a deep, sustained commitment to artistic ways of knowing and being. In doing so they have shown that the studio, or atelier, and the atelierista are at the heart of learning (Vecchi, 2010). Their work continues to remind us that learning has an aesthetic dimension and that beauty matters.

Howard Canatella (2006), Stuart Richmond (2004), Elaine Scarry (1999), and Joe Winston (2008) each propose that a delight in beauty should be at the core of education. The arts, Maxine Greene (1984) argues, are unique and necessary in that they transfigure the commonplace and open up unique dimensions. The languages and images we find in art "make perceptible, visible, and audible that which is no longer or not yet perceived, said, or heard in everyday life" (Marcuse, quoted in Greene, 1984, p. 129). The arts allow for a pedagogy of intensity and affect; they open us to the unexpected and the possibility of the "not yet" (see also Vecchi, 2010). It is impossible not to acknowledge that the work in Reggio Emilia has touched the bone, and the heart, of our project.

However, we started our project, and we wrote this book, in response to our concern with what is taking place in North American early childhood education with relation to Reggio Emilia's project. Our concern is in how the Reggio philosophy is often approached. In Reggio-inspired schools and practices, there is a tendency to try to make things look like Reggio rather than trying, as Lehrer describes, to figure out how things work. Perhaps there is nothing wrong with imitation. Many good ideas are born from copying, borrowing, or replicating, and as Scarry (1999) writes, these are some of the effects of beauty. She emphasizes that beauty has the ability to inspire and "brings copies of itself into being" (p. 3). But our interest is in doing more than simply bringing copies of Reggio into being—not just because the work has to find its own expression here, but because Reggio imitation frames the studio as something already known, with the process primarily implementing an already-known idea. Imitation misses the "not yet" of art.

Inviting Conversations Through Images

As a visual ethnography, images were central to our encounters with materials. We used images to open possibilities for different ways of knowing and to express and articulate thought. The visuals set the thinking in motion and our thought provoked the visuals. Yet in this book, we include very few of the hundreds of images we collected.

We have developed a companion website to the book that extends the ideas engaged in Chapters 2–6 through photos and film. Photography, film, and text are three events that allow us to create new terrains of engagement and to generate pedagogical possibilities. Each event requires different sensitivities and approaches, and each offers distinctive understandings of social realities. The question that framed the purpose of the companion website is the same as what we hoped to investigate in the project: How might we create worlds with images? For us, images offered an affective and aesthetic dimension that is also paramount in this book. Film and filming represented not just the act of seeing or the photographer's perspective, but a rich sensory, relational, gestural, and emotional experience. Photographs and other visual images on the website aid in understanding the nonverbal, the not easily articulated, the multimodal, the multidimensional. We invite readers to visit the website when reading the book: www.encounterswithmaterials.com.

By no means do the visuals act as an illustration of the narratives included in the book. Likewise, in both the book and on the companion website, the visuals are not records of what happened in our inquiries. We deliberately set out to pay attention to what paper, charcoal, paint, clay, and blocks might *do* and to imagine something other than meaning residing in children's understandings, words, and actions.

FIGURE 1.1   Through the eye of the camera

Sylvia Kind, Author

Associating photography with the real, tangible, objective world is in many respects a dangerous gaze. Photography is often understood to be an imprint of reality or an "unmediated copy of the real world" (Sturken & Cartwright, 2009, p. 17). Susan Sontag (1977), for instance, once described a photograph as "not only an image (as a painting is an image), an interpretation of the real; it is also a trace, something directly stenciled off the real, like footprints or a death mask" (p. 154).

One of the challenges we encountered in our project was to think outside of representation, of what images mean. Photography assumes a privileged relationship with and responsibility to reality because a photograph, particularly in film photography, acts as proof of an object's existence. The object must have been there, the event must have happened, or else "there would be no light reflected from it and no form for the negative to capture" (Navab, 2001, p. 76). A photograph, then, is evidence of a real, tangible world: It visualizes, or makes visible, something about the world as it is seen or experienced.

In early childhood contexts, we can see this idea of representation in practices where photography is used to help make visible a child's interior world and gain insight into children's lives, concerns, and experiences (Clark, 2005; Close, 2007; Richards, 2009; Thompson, 2008). While photos may reflect or in some way allude to what is happening in children's minds and lives, the representational focus tends to emphasize the passivity of the world and the agency of the subject who perceives. As Rose (2004) writes, it assumes that the "self" is the pole of activity, presence, and power and that the "other" is the pole of passivity (p. 20).

Whether a photograph is considered to be an accurate or even a constructed representation, the camera is most often considered a passive instrument or a tool in the hands of the photographer. The camera, a machine, does what it is programmed to do. To look through the lens is to objectively capture the world, and to be objective generally means detachment and disentanglement. But as Law (2004), discussing Haraway, writes, detachment is never possible because we are always caught up "in a dense material-semiotic network. . . . We are entangled in our flesh, in our versions of vision, and in relations of power that pass through and are articulated by us. So detachment is impossible" (p. 68).

In our research we did not use the camera as a passive machine, a "reasonable" tool, or an objective instrument. Each image in this book and on the website circulates in relation to other images, in relation to the viewer's own subjectivity and ways of seeing, and in relation to contexts, cultures, and histories. Images and objects are entangled in complex semiotic webs. We are interested, as Rose (2004) writes, in embracing "noisy and unruly processes capable of finding dialogue with each other and with the world . . . a dialogue that requires a 'we' who share a time and space of attentiveness" (p. 21). We see photography as a process of collaborating and moving *with* the world, a between-space, rather than a view from either outside or inside. As Haraway (1988) describes, we experiment with a vision that refuses indisputable recordings of what is simply there. Thus, our purpose in including photos from our ethnography in the book is to bring images into conversations. We work with the images as propositions for further experimentation. We engage in a process of diffraction.

Diffraction as a Mode of Inquiry

As it might have become clear to the reader by now, this book does not include reflections on the pedagogical moments that took place during the project. We do not recount what took place in those moments to understand children's meanings or to deconstruct pedagogies. We diffract.

Drawing on physicist Karen Barad's (2007, 2011) ideas, we work with diffraction, as opposed to reflection, as a way of thinking with materials in this book. Reflection is similar to *representationalism*—an idea we inherited from the Enlightenment. Representationalism is the belief that the world can be perfectly represented (reflected) through rigorous epistemological acts of Truth and the establishment of rigid boundaries delineating difference. In other words, Truth represents a single, neatly bounded Reality. Diffraction, by contrast, coincides with *performativity*, a direct material engagement with the world that does not hold subjects and objects strictly apart, but instead understands the world in intra-acting phenomena. Reflection and diffraction offer very different ways of looking at—or rather, being in and with—the world.

Because we find diffraction to be generative of thought, pedagogical moments within each chapter are not told in sequence as if they tell the story of what happened. They do not follow a logical structure. We do not analyze the moments for meaning, nor do we tell stories to be imitated. We produce something new with the pedagogical moments. We are interested in how the moments help us think differently about materials and materiality. How they help us make a difference. Create new worlds (Haraway, 2008). Shift our attention (Latour, 2005a). Generate thought through concepts.

Diffracting With Concepts

As Thiele (2014) explains, in a thought-practice, "concepts are not abstraction *from* the world, but an active force *of* this world—and thus always/already implicated in and concerned with world(ing): practicing *and* envisioning specific practices for this world" (p. 203, emphasis in original). As ways of worlding, these concepts are merely acts, not explanations. Brian Massumi (1987) reminds us that "a concept is a brick" that "can be used to build the courthouse of reason" or "can be thrown through the window" (p. 173). We hope the concepts and materials in this book do not become routines or procedures to master and repeat, but become invitations to think pedagogy otherwise. Invitations to create new concepts, to matter new worlds through materials. A concept, to paraphrase Stengers (2005), is a technique and a force of thinking that allows us to grasp new details and transform both ourselves and our modes of engagement.

The concepts we selected to think with are then connected to other concepts that help us extend our thoughts. All of these concepts have emerged from our theoretical inspirations. This book, like the project it emerged from, is inspired by the relational ontologies and more-than-human onto-epistemologies advanced by numerous environmental humanities scholars, philosophers, science studies researchers, anthropologists, cultural geographers, artists, and others (e.g., Barad, 2007, 2011; Bennett, 2004, 2010; Deleuze & Guattari, 1987; Haraway, 2008, 2015; Ingold, 2011, 2013; Law, 2004; Oates, n.d.; O'Sullivan, 2006; Puig de la Bellacasa, 2015; Rose, 2004; Springgay, 2011, 2012; Stengers, 2015; Tsing, 2005, 2011, 2012, 2013; van Dooren, 2014; van Dooren & Rose, forthcoming; Wolseley, 2016; Zhang, n.d., 2009) who want to change materials' humanist and capitalist story—a story that has entailed rampantly accumulating materials and then trashing them in quantities sufficient to poison and endanger our planet.

This Book's Entanglements With Paper, Charcoal, Paint, Clay, and Blocks

The book is organized by materials. Each chapter engages with a material that became important in the classrooms we collaborated with. Yet, the chapters do not explain the materials. Instead, each chapter connects itself (diffracts) to concepts to think about pedagogy differently with materials. Inspired by Thiele (2014), we *think-practice* with the materials as we write about them, following concepts in order to enable thought. The materials and the concepts are as follows:

- paper: movement
- charcoal: encounter
- paint: assemblage
- clay: ecologies
- blocks: time

In Chapter 2 we begin with the paper we write on to tell stories of how materials are caught up in the world's flows, rhythms, and intensities (Pacini-Ketchabaw, 2010). What do paper's versatility, variety, deceptive strength, and precarious fragility set in motion as paper interacts with the movements of the world? To explore this question, we attend to both the surface of paper and to paper as surface to generate moments with which to work and think. How might we

FIGURE 1.2 Tear, rip, paste, consider, sway

Sylvia Kind, Author

look at paper in ways that open our imaginations? How does paper play into our thinking? We pay attention to what paper does: sticking itself onto children's bodies, flying in the air of the classroom, freely venturing into hallways, blanketing surfaces, becoming particular (and not just being paper in its generality). We decide to play and exaggerate paper's ability to be caught up in the movement of air. Things happen: Children join in, as do we, as do trees, vents, fans. The paper responds. Everything and everyone responds. And new questions emerge.

We encounter charcoal in Chapter 3, and all of a sudden things become unrecognizable. We experiment with how charcoal covers and uncovers as a way of generating possibilities for telling stories in new ways. We wonder: How do we tell stories? What histories emerge in the ways we tell stories? What histories are not seen through the charcoal or our camera's lens? What marks does charcoal leave in the stories we tell? What marks are never uncovered? What is framed

FIGURE 1.3 Grind, crush, growl, howl, excavate, unearth

Sylvia Kind, Author

when charcoal covers and when things become uncovered? How can we tell stories through the residue charcoal leaves everywhere? For instance, we might tell stories differently if we wanted to recognize the marks charcoal leaves behind on bodies or in forests or in trees, nails, clothing, or in us, or in educators, or, or, or. And importantly, what does charcoal set in motion when we play with charcoal's movements of covering and uncovering?

Paint oozes through Chapter 4 and assembles new actions. Here we become interested in the invitations paint provokes and what is generated through them. How does paint invite other materials, and children, to respond? Paint on the floor, on easels, on walls, on bodies, on brushes invites different actions, different movements, different ways of being and becoming. How children and how other materials respond to paint's provocations also differs as each participates in the process. Nothing is predictable or set. Possibilities are endless. Yet, histories are

FIGURE 1.4   Mix, dab, stab, pat, stroke, flick, laugh

Sylvia Kind, Author

roused through these invitations, and these histories constrain and shape encounters with paint. We use these constraints as spaces of generation. Paint becomes an event that acts by materializing its viscosity, smoothness, and slipperiness throughout the classroom in relation to other things. Paint invites the reader to think with it and to do something with it.

Clay molds and shapes Chapter 5. Our interest here is when clay becomes clay, when a material becomes a material through its trajectory. We also want to discover how clay acts and interacts in ecologies: on the ground in the forest, when it is scooped from the river, when it enters the studio. We think about clay's demands: when we look at the final product that has been shaped, when the clay goes back to the earth after we have encountered it, when it responds to our movements as we work with it, when it refuses to stay still in one shape, when it flows through the studio in rhythm with children's movements, when it is cured through intense high heat. We follow the shapes that emerge as clay

FIGURE 1.5   Scrub, rub, wobble, trickle, melt

Sylvia Kind, Author

intra-acts with the children, the transformations clay constantly invites through its easy malleability and its ability to slow things down when it comes into contact with air and dries. We follow clay's unexpected movements as it interacts with shoes, with pockets, with hands, with boots, pine needles, water, rocks, twigs. As we follow clay, again, we generate questions.

Wooden blocks construct Chapter 6 as they become in interaction with time, sticks, tubes, chairs, buckets, plasticine, paper, children. We engage with two questions: What happens when we pay close attention to what blocks do? What does paying attention to blocks in interaction with other things set in motion? We quickly become curious about the stability and stationary condition of wooden blocks and begin to work with their movements to upset their stability. Attending to the ways blocks move and to the forces that constrain their movements, we cannot help but notice daily rhythms and the stillness and intensity of moments. Blocks move differently at different times, and time is lived differently with blocks. So time becomes another material to engage with.

Chapters 2 through 6 relate to and with each other. All the ideas are entangled. For instance, although Chapter 2 looks at paper through movement, the other concepts we engage are still at play. Chapter 3 looks at the concept of encounter through charcoal, but movement is still an important part of it. And so on. Thus, ideas repeat and concepts are interwoven, but particular things are brought more fully into view in each chapter.

The materials all come together in an afterword where we tell a brief story of the pedagogy of noticing. What happens when we notice and attend to materials' entanglements? What happens when we allow more and more things to enter our pedagogies? Might noticing materials in *relations* open possibilities for early childhood pedagogies?

FIGURE 1.6 Stack, clack, whack, knock, topple, fall, look

Sylvia Kind, Author

Now, we begin experimenting, inventing, playing with, and taking time to dwell with materials such as paper. As we played with paper, our thoughts took on its characteristics and became a lot like paper: transformable, not containable, flighty, at times airborne, malleable, multiplying, spreading. Paper became ordinary yet magical in its effects as educators and children joined together in movement.

2

PAPER

Movement

FIGURE 2.1 Materials live in the world in multiple ways

Sylvia Kind, Author

Paper flaps, floats, glides, hovers, soars, tears, rips, sways, flies, rolls, gathers, crumples, crimps, accepts, folds, bends, covers, swishes, flutters, pauses, bunches, scatters, yields. We breathe it in, we blow it out. We launch it, chew it, paste it, wear it, elevate it, wrap with it, read it, draw on it, flip it, collect it, paint it, propel it, drape it, color it. We open, envelop, fill, empty, catch, tie, write, arrange, twist, turn, rearrange, uncover, recover, unroll, wave, fasten, crinkle, tickle, clothe, amplify, circulate, sweep, undress, redress.

This chapter begins with paper: ordinary, everyday newspaper. *The Vancouver Sun*, to be precise. This local newspaper had been delivered every morning to houses, condos, and apartments; read once, sometimes two or three times; and then discarded in curbside recycling bins. We gathered several armloads of newspapers from these bins, enough to immerse ourselves in paper as we embarked on a journey of orienting ourselves to ways of being with materials with children. We started with "useless," "used-up," ordinary paper waiting to be removed and recycled. We interrupted this material's flow as it moved from bin to recycling depot. We wanted to try to understand paper, to understand what it might mean to be with paper, as we stepped into the flow of paper on its way from one place to another. We wondered: What if we think of paper as a material worthy of attention? A material with its own movements, histories, and possibilities? What if we think of paper as a material with potential to move us as we work with it?

So often, paper is regarded as a surface that we use to hold messages, lists, marks, meanings, drawings, paintings, stories, news. But after we have read the day's headlines, we no longer need the newspaper. Once a painting fills a page, it is dried, rolled, and stored inside a child's cubby until it is taken home. We wanted to interrupt this flow as well.

How do we get to know paper in other ways, in surprising ways? Tim Ingold (2011) writes of materials as riddles known through their stories. If paper is a riddle, what are its stories? To know paper in this way is not just to describe its properties or attributes, but to learn how it moves and to describe what happens to it as it shifts, mixes, modifies, mutates. Ingold emphasizes that materials are their verbs and their doings: We paper. We paint. And so we wanted to pay attention to materials' action words.

When we take paper into the studio to pay close attention to it, we find that nothing about it is static and everything is in motion. Things move, bodies move, materials move, the air moves, everything moves with a different rhythm and intensity. Life is filled with motion, new becomings, and emergences. Movements may be felt, observed, dramatic, collective, choreographed, barely perceptible. There are movements toward and movements away, movement as emergence—what comes of these moments and what is produced. There is movement as acting and as being acted on. In learning materials' movements and doings, we find our way to asking other questions. We learn to move with the materials and attend to the ways we are moved in response. We learn that learning itself is movement.

Singularity

Eli sits at the table in front of a wet papier-mâché bowl. He carefully smooths slippery paste over one long rectangle of newspaper and gently pats it into place on the bowl. He pauses, considers its placement, and then pulls it off, turns it over and around, pauses again, examines the piece, and reorients it to another spot. We notice his acute observation, the measured contact between hand, bowl, paper strip; paste drying and constricting on hands; paper sticking and coming loose. Eli appears to be drawn by particular strips of paper. He touches and lifts certain ones, searching their surfaces, responding to the curve of the bowl in a rhythmic and concentrated interplay of hands, turning bowl, paper strip, glue, breath. His breath is slow, and our own breath slows in response. If this were a musical piece, it would be the deep, resonant playing of a cello, the movements of bow on string elongated and extended. We breathe deeper as we follow Eli's intimate attention to each paper strip's singularity.

We started our paper experiments with newspaper because it was abundant and easy to find. It had not been purchased new as if it were "empty" and awaiting inscription. This newspaper had already had a life and a purpose. It had been in people's homes, dropped in mail slots, held in hands, perhaps read over morning coffee, taken to work and cafés before being discarded. It had not been produced for children's use, and although it was familiar to many of the children, the content of the news items was not fully available to this group of toddlers. Yes, they could make meaning of the pictures and occasionally recognize a letter or a number, but they did not regard the newspaper in a normative manner. Rather, they were drawn into the particular. Not a newspaper as a thing and not paper in general, but specific bits of paper in particular situations. A singular piece, a singular situation.

One morning there is a delightful rush of activity in the studio as mountains of newspaper strips are placed into clear plastic tubs in preparation for making papier-mâché. Kale climbs into a tub filled with newspaper strips. Paper strips cover his legs and torso, tickle his knees as children scoop more paper strips and empty them into the bin. Kale squirms in response and the children laugh, running to collect more strips. Paper takes flight, alights in the bin, and settles all around the sides. Like water filling a bathtub, the level of paper rises in Kale's tub. By now, paper covers the floor, litters children's hair, drifts through the studio. "Don't forget that one," Kale says, pointing across the room. Paper strips are everywhere, but we follow Kale's finger as he points to one long, wavy strip.

The paper, in its singularity, posed a puzzle to the children and the educators: What was this paper? Why was it here? What was it for? What could be done with it? What could it become? We wanted to find out. So we began with ordinary materials already in motion, and we followed children's movements: The turn of a hand, the flick of a finger, the rise and fall of the body's breath, the tearing of a narrow strip of paper drew us to notice each scrap and every subtle movement. Mihaly Csikszentmihalyi (1990) describes moments like these as "flow": bodies, materials, thoughts, and breath move together outside of time. Soon we were noticing the rhythms and flows of making, of bodied sensations, of how we were affected by the movements of making.

The Movements of Making

In early childhood, materials are closely connected to making. They are often set out for children to make or create something with, frequently with the assumption that children are full of ideas just waiting to be expressed through these materials. Yet, as Hillevi Lenz Taguchi (2010) describes, "the material world acts on our thinking as much as our thinking acts on the material world" (p. 49). We are moved by materials and are prompted by the materials' own characteristics and liveliness. It is never as simple as idea directly imposed on form.

Making, then, whether it results in an actual object or is engaged in as a series of events, involves an alchemic process of developing a rhythm and feel for the material (Ingold, 2013). Ingold (2011, 2013), relying on Elkins, describes alchemy as the ancient practice of struggling with materials—finding out what happens to them, what they feel and look like—and learning to follow them as they are mixed, heated, cooled, or combined with other elements and materials. The alchemy of paint, for instance, involves "bring[ing] together, into a single movement, a certain material mixture, loaded onto the brush, with a certain bodily gesture enacted through the hand that [holds] it" (Elkins, cited in Ingold, 2013, p. 28). In this way "a material is known not by what it is but by what it does" (Ingold, 2013, p. 29) and making includes a multitude of movements and gestures.

A group of children gathers in front of the clear glass studio door with a container of water and a large bowl filled with paper strips. One by one, they dip a strip of paper in the water and apply it to the door's transparent surface. The warm morning light streams in through the glass, speeding the paper's drying. Some strips fall off while others adhere. The educators join in the rhythm of figuring out the relationship of glass, water, paper, light, and temperature. Too little liquid and the paper won't stick; too much and it slides down; just enough and it is held in place.

Dónal O'Donoghue (2015), citing Eve Sedgwick, describes making as a three-way conversation with a material: "What will it let me do?" "What does it want to do?" "What is it that I want to do?" (p. 107). "These tugs, pulls, pushes and heaves," O'Donoghue (2015) writes, "these acts of giving, receiving, taking and being taken; these opportunities to go places conceptually, instinctually, intellectually, and affectively" (p. 107) are constant negotiations and movements.

Paper has its own inclinations. It acts on and with the water, with the walls, the floors, the door, and the children's bodies. It becomes known by how it floats; how it gets slimy; how it attaches under different conditions to walls, windows, and legs; how it feels; how it slips off; what it does; how it moves. Paper becomes known as receptive, reactive, pliant, absorbent, responsive to touch, to bending, folding, and crumpling. These movements may be subtle, yet working with paper means one moves with the material in continuous motion, joining forces with it (Ingold, 2013), responding to its inclinations. One thing leads to another, Ingold writes, in "a gestural dance with a modulation of the material" (2013, p. 26). One never quite knows where one will end up.

> *The studio is filled with newspaper strips. Some are in bins; some are stuffed into large, freestanding clear acrylic tubes; and countless others lie scattered on the floor. Kale is sitting on the floor near a shallow container of papier-mâché liquid. He picks up a single paper strip and dips it into the liquid. The paper initially floats, then becomes receptive to the liquid, and soon feels slippery to the touch. The longer it remains in the liquid the slimier it becomes. As Kale's fingers meet paper and paper meets liquid, something is suggested. Kale tests out this alchemy as he drapes one strip over his leg and momentarily pauses. It seems to feel pleasant to him. Impulsively he covers his leg with more soaked strips in a fluid movement between fingers, paper strip, liquid, and leg. The paper is slippery, cold, on his skin, and it soon draws other children and educators around to watch what is happening. Before long, other hands dip the paper in the liquid, pass the strips to Kale, and join in his experimentation.*

Continuous Motion

In thinking about making, it would be a mistake to think these movements are sequential or continuous in a linear sense. Or that paper is played with, materials are explored, and through a series of gestures and movements a goal is reached. Or that the process of working with a material leads us from one state to another and ends when a child becomes a dragon, when an object is made, or when a leg is covered. Instead, these movements are recursive, acting on each other in a continuous exchange back and forth. They reverberate and continue long after something is made.

> *An educator sweeps up at the end of the morning, and a few paper strips get caught in the movement of the broom and escape from the bag. There is a look, a hesitation, and the bag is overturned. Hundreds of strips join the few that escaped, and the children are pulled into a paper-sweeping game.*

Movement with paper is both rhythm and repetition—the doing and undoing—filling, emptying, sweeping, covering, uncovering. We see a desire to keep things in motion. Not a conscious desire per se. It is a desire that resembles life's movements, as Deleuze (1997, para. G2) explains: "Desire does not comprise any lack; neither is it a natural given"; "it is process, in contrast with structure or genesis; it is affect, as opposed to feeling; it is 'haecceity' (individuality of a day, a season, a life)"; "it is event, as opposed to thing or person"; it is "defined by zones of intensity, thresholds, gradients, flux."

> *A large purple exercise ball is perched on an upturned stool, inviting connections of paper strips and papier-mâché liquid. For weeks the children play with rhythms of covering and uncovering. Strip by strip, paper is dipped in the liquid and the ball is covered until its round surface resembles a paper moon. But it doesn't stay this way. Once covered, the moon is undone, paper kept in motion. Piece by piece, the strips are pulled off until the ball is visible again and the sticky paper strips are marshaled for other uses. Then one day there is a pause. The fire alarm rings. We are interrupted, and finally the ball stays covered. The paper strips constrict as they dry, and a half-moon shape is cut away from the purple ball, the moon becoming a paper bowl. It is carried around, temporarily becoming a hat, a shelter, a carry-all, a boat, a tub, a hiding place. It evolves as it responds to hands, air, temperature, feet. Paper strips separate, small tears form as the bowl moves throughout the room, coming undone. This paper is still in the process of becoming something else.*

Artist Andy Goldsworthy works with such movements in a similar way. He considers his creations as transient or ephemeral. Goldsworthy (n.d.) says, "I want my art to be sensitive and alert to changes in material, season and weather. Each work grows, stays, decays. Process and decay are implicit. Transience in my work reflects what I find in nature" (para. 4). Just as for Goldsworthy, for us working with paper was working through impermanence, continuously in motion. We had to resist "perfection" and static renderings.

Instead we became participants with the intensities and flows of materials in motion.

Caught in the Currents

Kale and Grayson take armloads of paper strips from the studio table to play games of shaking, throwing, crawling under the falling paper—arms outstretched as if to soar with the paper taking flight. We amplify the children's actions in response, echoing their movements and exaggerating the game by bringing a fan to play along. Having noticed how paper slips under the door into the hallway at the end of each day, we respond by hanging paper strips from the ceiling, hoping they will catch the movement of the air and trying to make these movements of paper and air more visible. When the children come into the studio in the morning, they are greeted by a light breeze generated by a floor fan. Narrow translucent wax paper strips hang from the ceiling, stirring with the movements of bodies and the circulating breeze.

Whenever we encounter a material, it is a material in movement. Paper yellows and fades over time, warps and curls with humidity, becomes more brittle, and shifts in the breeze or with the movement of bodies in a room. Paper hanging from the ceiling falls down with the drying of the tape that holds it in place, or with the slow weight of gravity. We work with paper as active, agentic, and dynamic. We learn that "materials are always and already on their ways to becoming something else" (Ingold, 2013; relying on Barad, 2013, p. 31).

In our studio, paper became caught up in the movements of the world, the movements of the air, the currents of the lifeworld. We wanted to exaggerate and amplify these movements by bringing in the fan, by working outside in the wind and on top of an outdoor vent. We became interested in the energy of the material itself. Inspired by Goldsworthy's art, we attended to "the energy and space around" paper as much as "the energy and space within" paper.

Ingold (2013) reminds us that we are participants in a world of active materials: "The conduct of thought goes along with, and continually answers to, the fluxes and flows of the materials we work with" (n.p.). Paper started to "think in us" as we started to "think through" it. In other words, we set up a "new" relation with the world, a relation of what Ingold calls correspondence. In this new relation, we attempted to better respond *with* the world, rather than accumulating tons of information *about* the world (Ingold, 2013). This correspondence opened possibilities of being taken by surprise.

Surprise (Being Moved by the Materials)

Teachers and children have gathered outdoors around a large, rectangular raised cement structure covered by a heavy grill. From somewhere deep inside the structure, a fan generates a strong upward gust of air. We place the papier-mâché bowls we made a couple of weeks ago (little ones, middle ones, huge ones) on top of the grill. The paper bowls hover, glide, soar, and fly! Bodies move in concert with the flow of air and the traveling bowls. Surprised by the movement of the bowls in the wind, Mira bends into one little bowl's line of flight as she sends it across the grill to the children on the other side. "You have to move with it," she says, her arms echoing gestures of releasing the bowl and its floating action as it moves across the grill.

The littlest bowl is named Baby. "Baby! Come here, Baby!" Sophia sings with arms outstretched while her fingers beckon. She calls out again: "Baby, come here! Come here, Baby!" The bowl unexpectedly responds as it catches the flow of air and floats toward her. "I got it!" she cries and holds it close in an embrace before it takes flight again on the currents of the wind. Everything moves together in synchronicity: voices calling, hands outstretched, air gusting, a child's desire, the baby bowl, and all the bodies. Even the wind rustling through the surrounding trees seems to be joining in.

We are surprised by how this encounter is taking shape as a slow dance. Bodies, bowls, arms, paper strips, and wind move together, in and out. This collective experience brings an unexplainable delight: the delight of being moved by materials.

What surprised us most was that after we learned to follow its movements, paper wove itself into our lifeworlds. And when this happened, we were encouraged to dream with paper, or, as Ingold says, to see things in the way paper lives in the world. Our practice somehow became what Davies (2014) refers to as "emergent listening," opening itself up to "the possibility of new ways of knowing and new ways of being" (p. 21) so that something new and surprising can happen.

Movement Across

The collective experience of paper bowls flying across the vent presented other possibilities of being with materials and with each other—not only for the children, but also for the educators. Some time after the paper experience was over, Sylvia and some of the educators visited the New Media Art Gallery in New Westminster, British Columbia, to see Karina Smigla-Bobinski's work, ADA,

a visitor-animated interactive art-making machine (http://www.smigla-bobinski.
com/english/works/ADA/index.html). The artist had created a huge helium-
filled transparent spherical balloon with thick charcoal sticks protruding in even
intervals all around the circumference. It was enclosed and floating in a rectangular white room, the surfaces of which had become densely marked by the
black charcoal. One only had to enter the room to see that something was
happening. The most relevant questions were not about ADA's meaning or
symbolic function, or what this installation was, but what it could do, what
could happen, and what we could do in the midst of it. Visitors could walk in
through an entryway and interact with ADA, so we went in and began to play
with her. We could take hold of the charcoal protrusions and play with her
resistances, the weight or pressure of air pushing against the desires of one's arms
to move this "machine" fast and make long strokes on the walls, trying to get
into corners and extend beyond the boundaries of the existing marks. Or we
could gently nudge the ball and move with its slow movements, batting back
and forth, hands softly pushing her into the wall, moving in concert with her
placid gliding as she floated out from the walls and drifted up toward the ceiling. We could work with or against ADA's own inclinations.

Being surrounded by the rich black lines and marks on the ceiling, walls, and
floor, feeling the movements of the ball as it bounced from surface to surface,
being in the midst of it was a moving experience: an emotional, bodied, tactile,
sensory, *felt* experience. We felt delight in the pleasure of the experience and a
desire to move with it. The experience echoed what O'Sullivan (2006) describes:
that affect is not about an individual but a collective; it has more to do with an
experience than with representation. That is, the experience of being in the
charcoal-marked room, playing with and finding ourselves moving with ADA,
and getting to know some of ADA's potentiality, like the experience of gathering
around the outdoor vent and being caught up in the play of paper, bodies, and
wind, is the point of the work: finding oneself moved by the experience. It can
spill out, affect others, and offer new ways of being in the world (O'Sullivan,
2006).

While we were at the gallery experiencing ADA, we watched a man and two
children enter the room. The man waited at the door while his young children
interacted with ADA. As they ran to him with blackened hands and arms outstretched as if to greet him and draw him in, he drew back several steps and
extended his hands in a gesture of "stay back!" To stay back affirms charcoal's
messiness, affirms a drawing and bouncing ball as child's play, and reconfirms
the separation between the life and desires of a child and those of an adult.

O'Donoghue (2015) discusses this turn to experience in contemporary art.
He describes how artists who are committed to art production that is participatory, interactive, and collaborative have conceptualized and pursued experience
as an essential element of their work, creating situations and putting conditions
into play so that the artwork *is* the experience or produces an experience, rather

than being a representation or translation of an already lived experience. Here O'Donoghue relies on Dewey (1916), who emphasizes the immediacy of experience and the interconnected processes of "doing and undergoing" (p. 46). According to Dewey, an artistic experience is a dynamic and fluid one of acting, responding, making, considering, creating, experimenting, forming, and transforming. As a collective productive participatory experience. There is a lively fullness of experience and affective, sensory, bodied, holistic engagements.

Perhaps, we thought, our response to children might be about organizing experience to produce joyful encounters, or, as O'Sullivan (2006) says, those which "increase our capacity to act in the world" (p. 42). O'Donoghue (2015) refers to this role of a teacher as *experience-producers* who create opportunities for dwelling in the world, for experiencing that which "may not seem possible until lived" (pp. 105–106).

Paper in Its Final Move

Paper was the experience of it, the doing of paper, the moving with paper. As researchers, we noticed how things move together, how the material experimentations became a choreography of children, educators, bodies, materials, places, histories, stories intersecting, interacting, influencing, and working together. There were rhythmic movements of doing and undoing, pleasures of gathering and dispersing, composing and decomposing and of keeping things in motion. We noticed how children looked for opportunities to take things apart, how they intervened in their own work to undo, loosen, and take apart so they could keep the work going. We noticed rhythms of pause and engagement, these pauses a pivot. These forces, flows, and movements are akin to Tim Ingold's (2013) description of improvisation: a rhythmic quality of working with the ways of the world. There was never *iteration*, a repetition or re-presentation of the world, but *itineration* as everyone and everything joined with the forces and flows of the world.

As paper moves through time and with the world, it encounters other materials.

3

CHARCOAL

Encounter

FIGURE 3.1   What marks does charcoal leave in the stories we tell?
Sylvia Kind, Author

Approach, grind, crush, pursue, disguise, climb, blaze, howl, growl, sing, extract, unearth, dig, discover, excavate, mark, saw, cut, wrap, burn, roast, draw, darken, smudge, conceal, reveal, sift, hesitate, draw in, shake, pulverize, hammer, thump, transfer, try, pour, examine, uncover, cover, draw near, disperse, handle, grate, chop, spread, sweep, dust, brush, multiply, stroke, encompass, draw together, wound, attend, heal, dispense, barter, sell, extrapolate, undo, recover, remark, return, redo.

We searched the forest for blackened trees burned by long-ago fires and collected their charred offerings. We gathered branches and prepared them for burning. We sang around a copper fire bowl as we roasted vegetables, making our own charcoal. We drew together with charcoal, both purchased and from the fire. We created large studio-events of investigating, crushing, gathering, sifting, and dispersing charcoal fragments. We were covered. We uncovered. We recovered from the covering and the uncovering.

Traces of charcoal remain in our memories, ground into our clothes. Traces remain in the expectation charcoal still generates long after our experimentations. Charcoal-smudged communion dresses still hang in the studio; sticks are still gathered in anticipation of another fire. We carry traces of the forest, the wood, the fire, the gathering, crushing, drawing, burning, marking, blackness, dust. The damp earthy smells of the trees.

Charcoal is a thing: a stick of compressed burned wood. But it is also a continuum, a story, an event, a happening, a doing. We are interested in charcoalness, the expression and experience of charcoal in the encounter: always in process, always becoming charcoal. This "isness" (Springgay, 2011, 2012) of a thing disrupts stillness. Charcoal is not just for drawing with.

Charcoal still holds hope.

We think about an encounter as a moment of meeting, where things and forces and human and nonhuman beings come together in spaces of difference. In this meeting we decide how to respond—whether to follow, join with, intervene, provoke, perhaps work against. Something is set in motion in the encounter. An encounter emphasizes the collective and the relational, not individual experience.

And a moment, according to Massumi (2002), is what you are compelled to pay attention to. There is immediacy in the moment, a sensory, sensational (Springgay, 2011, 2012) attending-to. We are talking here of a relational encounter, not of an object of recognition. Things connect tangentially, shooting off in many directions. Nothing is reconfirmed in an encounter. The world is not already known. Confirmation and knowledge are the domains of recognition. O'Sullivan (2006) notes that in recognition, "we and the world we inhabit are reconfirmed as that which we already understood our world and ourselves to be" (p. 1). Unlike a recognition, an encounter disrupts the "*re*presentation of something always already in place: our habitual way of being and acting in the world" (p. 1, emphasis in original).

In a genuine encounter, our usual ways of being in the world are confronted and challenged, our knowledge systems disrupted: "We are forced to thought" (O'Sullivan, 2006, p. 1). An encounter, according to Deleuze and Guattari (1987), always disturbs.

This chapter considers moments of encounter where finger meets charcoal, charcoal meets skin, blackness meets mirror, wood meets fire, and something unexpected and generative takes place. We consider what happens, what is set in motion, when forces meet-touch-attend-open-respond.

To Meet

We are sitting around a table in the early childhood center, drawing together with charcoal. Some of the charcoal pieces have been gathered from burnt trees during our adventures in the forest, and some have been purchased from the local edu-cational supply store. Sheets of white paper are spread out in front of the children, and a lively, intermittent conversation touches on wood, trees, bonfires, how to draw tanks and trucks, bushwhacking, tank stickers, gargoyles, how charcoal might have come to be in the forest. Nerissa falls silent. With a slow, rhythmic move-ment of her body, she marks the paper, studies her hands becoming receptive to the blackness, and smudges careful charcoal lines on her hands. Noticing how the charcoal migrates to her hands and arms, she responds to these marks, to the talk around the table, to the paper-becoming-black. Her paper is soon filled with dense black lines in rhythm with her hands and arms becoming blacker and blacker until they are covered up to her elbows with soft, rich, chalky darkness. She smiles and finally looks up at the others around her, holds up her hands like small claws. With a hint of surprise in her voice, she tells the others she is becoming a gargoyle.

To meet in spaces of difference means we cannot anticipate or predict what something is, what something means, what will or should happen. Rather than knowing ahead of time what certain materials might do or what they might be for, rather than "allowing" children time and space to discover that which has already been discovered or is predetermined, an encounter is marked by a certain kind of expectation: a hopeful, watchful attention to what might emerge. For instance, we might set aside time for children to explore charcoal and the kinds of marks it makes. While our planning allows for a valuable aspect of getting to know the material, there is a tendency for our expectations, or our previously held understandings, to frame and con-strain what takes place: that charcoal makes particular marks, that charcoal is for drawing.

Instead of planning or expecting, an encounter looks for the not yet known. It is marked by a sense of *not knowing*, of hopeful waiting. A material is not defined by what *I know* about it. Things could always become other things. Even in a space set aside for drawing with charcoal, drawing could be something other than what we understand it to be. Charcoal could become something other than a drawing instrument. Paper could be more than a surface. We make an effort to perceive what we haven't yet imagined, to see what lies beyond our field of vision.

The classroom is quiet and scattered with the residue of charcoal pastel on paper, on walls, on carpet. Mariam and Joe enter the room and it comes to life. Picking up charcoal-marked paper from the floor and covering themselves, they exclaim, "We need tape!" The tape arrives and the children wrap themselves tightly with the charcoal "costumes." They are monsters now, running around the classroom. Four other children join in, and soon everyone is covered with charcoal.

An encounter is interested in the new—new ways of perceiving and acting with and in the world, unexpected relations, transversal connections. New does not necessarily mean original. It is not an obsession with the novel. New is what might emerge unexpectedly in an encounter. New means meeting, always for the first time, even if the "meeters" have met a hundred times, in spaces of difference.

To meet in spaces of difference requires hospitality and openness to the other. Charcoal is intensely hospitable to encounters with others. It marks, spreads, covers, envelops, draws in. As it does this, it announces its presence and compels a response. It is difficult to remain neutral to charcoal and unaffected by it. Charcoal's rich blackness, its infinite tiny particles, its chalky softness compels, repels, affronts.

Such hospitality is imbued with the act of listening. Bronwyn Davies (2014) says that "encounters with others lie at the heart of listening—and of life itself" (p. 5). She writes:

> Listening is about being open to being affected. It is about being open to difference, and, in particular, to difference in all its multiplicity as it emerges in each moment in between oneself and another. Listening is about *not* being bound by what you already know. It is life as movement.
>
> *(p. 1, emphasis in original)*

Encounters with others, Davies suggests, "where each is open to being affected by the other" (p. 1), are integral to life itself.

The room is quiet. Only a few child-bodies remain after the others have left the room to get ready for snack. On the floor, a large sheet of once-white paper is now a deep, rich black, covered with traces of the pastel charcoal presented to the children that morning. Martin and Ziri are rolling back and forth on the paper. The paper, the charcoal, and the bodies become one—boundaries blur as the bodies are covered in charcoal and the charcoal merges with the bodies. Blake's "The Snowman, Walking in the Air" plays softly in the background.

To meet and listen in an encounter is, as Paulina Rautio (2013) proposes, "an occasion to ask: what is it that takes place in the moment" (p. 399)? It is an education of attention, and of affirmation. It is hope and expectation—anticipating being moved and affected. Melora Koepke (2015) writes that "a pedagogy of moments seeks to have the infinite possibilities of existence narrowed down into the enunciation of the present, with the objects and experiences that are at hand" (para. 7). It's not oriented toward results, or what should happen, but toward "fields of possibility" (para. 13). To meet and to listen is to attend to this moment of meeting: "ungraspable in its moment of occurrence, but real in its effects" (O'Sullivan, 2006, p. 21).

Being hospitable comes with the hope of being disoriented, of not being able to make sense. It is rupture: moments of problem posing (Koepke, 2015). It is curating experiences that undo us, cultivating wonder in the unknown, creating situations that make us uncomfortable so that genuine encounters might take place and something new might emerge.

These practices are not "wild destratification" (O'Sullivan, 2006, p. 33), however. It is not an "anything goes" approach. It is thought-full, intentional, and careful attention to what is taking place and what is emerging in the in-between.

To Touch

To touch charcoal is to gesture toward it. Erin Manning (2007) describes touch as a gesture of turning toward or reaching toward, a movement, a tenuous, ephemeral exposure of oneself to the other—not the already-known other, but the other that just might emerge in the exchange. Potentiality—who one might be or what things might become—is at the heart of this gesture (p. 7). Touch invents, she says, "by drawing the other into relation" (p. xiv). In her words,

> To touch is always to touch something, someone. I touch not by accident, but with a determination to feel you, to reach you, to be affected by you. Touch implies a transitive verb, it implies that I *can*, that I *will* reach toward

you and allow the texture of your body to make an imprint on mine. Touch produces an event.

(p. 12)

To touch charcoal is to be touched, to be affected, to be moved. As Manning (2007) explains, "I cannot touch you without being responsive" (p. 9). To touch charcoal as Nerissa did, for instance, or as Martin and Ziri did, is to be touched by it, to be open to a multitude of possibilities of who one might become, of what the charcoal-drawing-blackness might become.

Charcoal touched us.

To touch is to attend to the body (Manning & Massumi, 2014), to the ways bodies move. Manning (2007) locates touch

as one way of thinking this body-in-movement. This is not to give touch preferential treatment . . . touch is to be understood synesthetically, operating along relational vectors always in dialogue with other senses (of which there are likely more than five). To think touch synesthetically is to appreciate all of the ways in which movement alters the body.

(p. xiii)

During our year of experimenting with charcoal, we—educators, researcher, and children—visited Unfolding, a retrospective of the work of South Korean-born conceptual artist Kimsooja. Her work engages with everyday objects, the acts of sewing, and the daily life of textiles. As we entered the exhibit we encountered a room where long fabric panels hung, as if from a series of clotheslines. As we walked through the room, the vibrantly colored silk swayed and brushed against our bodies: pinks, yellows, and reds reflected and multiplied along the mirror-lined walls. It was impossible not to touch and be touched by the fabric. A multiplicity of senses and connections combined, layered, infused, overlapped, so that touching was more than the physical act of skin on matter. It became a receptive turning toward.

For Erin Manning, "the proposition is that touch—every act of reaching toward—enables the creation of worlds. This production is relational. I reach out to touch you in order to invent a relation that will, in turn, invent me" (2007, p. xv). In our experimentations, charcoal produced new visceral bodily relations. Bodies in action: doing, making, becoming. Bodies in process through sensations. Grosz (2008, cited in Springgay, 2012) writes that "sensation impacts the body, not through the brain, not through representations, signs, images, or fantasies, but directly on the body's own internal forces, on cells, organs, the nervous system" (p. 73).

Veronica's camera zooms in on Ziri, who is lying motionless on the paper with arms and legs extended. His open eyes are directed at the ceiling, but we're almost certain they do not see. The palms of his hands press on the charcoal-paper-floor, fingers extended. Slowly, his legs and arms start moving in rhythmic snow-angel motions. After a few seconds, he rises to his knees and puts his ear to the charcoal-paper so he can hear what the charcoal is saying. On his back again, he moves his snow-angel arms and legs on the paper. Then he crawls across the paper, feeling its texture beneath his knees and hands. More snow-angel making and he gets up again, this time to show the educator his charcoal-covered hands. On the paper again, snow-angel movements. This back and forth continues for more than ten minutes. Every snow-angel motion is coupled with another action: Ziri jumps like a frog; he circles the paper; he rolls.

To Attend

To attend is to notice the world around us, including its heterogeneity (Tsing, 2011). Practicing attunement requires awareness of the in-between, attending to the relations between things. It is akin to van Dooren and Rose's (forthcoming) "ethical practice of 'becoming-witness' which seeks to explore and respond to others in the fullness of their particular 'ethos,' or way of life" (para. 1). Paying attention "invites us into a sense of wonder" (van Dooren, 2014, p. 8), of opening ourselves up to the world we are part of.

One morning we take out the large copper fire bowl and prepare for a charcoal-burning-veggie-roasting-campfire outside the early childhood center. Our intention is to make charcoal out of the sticks we had gathered in the forest. Sitting around the fire bowl, we find ourselves lingering in the midst of camping stories, children singing, dappled light, rhythms of sharpening roasting sticks, pungent smells of campfire and veggies roasting, scraping sounds of newly burned charcoal sticks on the sidewalk. This encounter has no goals. It is a leisurely coming-together of wood and fire and children and light and vegetables and all the potentialities of our lingering.

To attend to something means to pause. To linger with, dwell in, take time with. As Kimmerer (2003) writes, "attentiveness alone can rival the most powerful magnifying glass" (p. 8). Yet this attentiveness is not about looking at the thing per se or observing the children's actions, but pausing in the relations between. Being attentive is to take time with the "chaotic and vibratory spaces of activeness that are co and re-composed" in the world (Springgay, 2012, p. 557). For us, to attend involved creating conditions to linger, let go, stretch out, and open our minds and eyes to see that anything can connect to anything else.

To Open

> *We are in the forest collecting charcoal from blackened trees burned in a fire that swept through the area long ago. The children gather, grind, sift, and experiment with the charred remains. They saw fallen branches with hand-held graters and gather sawdust into jars. A few try to grate the root of a living cedar and are surprised when curious white patches edged with red appear. Zoey slowly runs her finger over the patches, probing their smooth surface. Caleb poses questions to the others: "Are the trees alive? How alive are they? Is this their blood and bones? Are they humans? Can they talk?" The children check for a heartbeat. Hearing nothing, they turn away and continue grating. But then we see the tree's wound, the "blood" and "bones." We hear the hierarchies of aliveness, and we are undone. What is happening here?*

Atkinson (2011) suggests that "allowing oneself to become undone is a crucial condition for learning" (p. 165). To be undone by a wound to a tree or by the blackness of bodies is a powerful and risky thing. It means not approaching things as if we need to fix, make "right," or limit so that only that which we have previously determined to be acceptable or "good" will take place. Rather, it is necessary to allow ourselves to be undone and to attend to that which "undoes" us.

An encounter, O'Sullivan (2006) notes, "operates as a rupture in our habitual modes of being and thus in our habitual subjectivities" (p. 1). Every encounter produces a "cut," or a crack, he says. Yet, it also holds "a moment of affirmation, the affirmation of a new world" (p. 1). It holds "a way of seeing and thinking this world differently" (p. 1) and requiring "us to think otherwise" (p. 1).

Thinking is a practice that takes center stage in our early childhood centers. This is not a cerebral thinking. Thinking for us is about cultivating wonder and opening to encounters in order to unsettle, disturb, or move them (Davies, 2014). Dahlberg and Moss (2005), draw from Deleuze suggest that in early childhood education knowledge is "a dull concept, almost deadly, leading nowhere; it is about recognition of existing facts and the solution of known problems" (p. 114). They contrast knowledge with the concept of thought, and liken thought to life: "Thought opens up—to change, innovation, invention of new possibilities. Thought is critical and creative—of new concepts, problems, and learning" (p. 114).

Several four-year-old girls enter the studio and gather around the long, paper-covered tables holding collections of charcoal sticks in small porcelain dishes. The charcoal draws them in, and the girls experiment with making marks on the paper. Meandering, inquisitive lines go far, while short strokes pressed hard into the paper leave black crumbs. As the children draw, the charcoal travels, spreading over the paper and covering fingers and hands. Paper and skin are receptive to charcoal's soft blackness. After the first few tentative marks and noticeable pleasure in the spreading charcoal, the encounter unfolds quickly. Finger meets charcoal, blackness meets skin, charcoal meets story. Fairy tales, movie scenes, gendered discourses of romance and growing older, chairs that had been pushed against the wall to make way for the charcoal event all intertwine. Charcoal becomes makeup. Chairs become a bus. It is as if everything is thrown into the air (Olssen, 2009) and is combined and recombined in unexpected ways. We linger for a while to take note of the many things at play here, our hesitation playing in the erupting encounters as well. By this time the children, nearly fully blackened by the soft charcoal dust, are sitting on the bus going to a ball to meet the black prince.

In our daily work, we opened ourselves to experimentation (Kind & Pacini-Ketchabaw, 2016), in particular, to experimentation as a complex social-affective-political phenomenon. Our intention was always to rupture the romance of experimentation, of the beautiful, of the exotic. Experimenting has the potential to bring life to sedimented discourses. It aims to increase our capacity to act in the world, to produce new forms of life (see O'Sullivan, 2006, p. 78), and to open up perceptions and understandings. This is always a risky endeavor.

In opening to experimentation, we engage with children, materials, narratives, and situations as they act on and act with each other and enter into complex, entangled networks and assemblages. It is not just human relationality. It is about the capacity for things and beings to respond to each other in space, in and out of time, in movement, in an environment that allows for multiple convergences and intersections. In experimentation, we get to know the power, possibilities, and consequences of a material. We work within the tensions and ethics of listening to children's own concerns as we attend to the materials and discourses they play with. We become witness to how children take the substance of their lives—including the circulating images, narratives, and ideas—and make something of them, inventing, reproducing, transforming. We are interested in what children select, what they choose as desirable, what a material such as charcoal can bring into play. Yet experimentation is not innocent as if it only involves children's creative inventions. It is not "free" experimentation without any obligations or response-abilities (Haraway, 2008). And so we respond.

To Respond

We are in the early childhood center preparing wood we had gathered from the forest for the charcoal-burning event. At one end of the room, a few children are using a hand-held saw to divide a long willow branch into smaller pieces. Others are at tables using scissors to cut cedar, fir, alder, and other willow-wood twigs into lengths so they can be wrapped in foil and placed in the fire. Scissors, saw, and children's hands cannot cut wood quickly or easily, so it takes time, and we linger together with the severed pieces, the scent of the wood, peeling bark, crinkling foil, and a dozen different trajectories of cutting, breaking, wrapping, covering. Jayden, bringing scissors to twig, notices a tiny bug crawling over the bark. He gently carries the bug outside to set it free. Still concerned that we might be about to burn a bug's home, he writes a thank-you note to the branch and tapes it onto the wrapped-around foil. Later, when we are gathered around the fire, there is a momentary pause in the laughter and activity as we silently watch the flames engulf Jayden's letter.

To respond in our creative eruptions was a way of learning to move with, not passively observe, highly charged events, to be open to being moved and to act, to engage with emerging propositions and step into emerging choreographies. To *do* something in concert with the movements. To find ways to play along. This is akin to Haraway's (2008) *response-ability*: It is more than acknowledging the other or following rules. Response-ability is about sharing and feeling in the moment, whether it is a moment of joy or a moment of suffering. Paulina Rautio (2013) writes that "even if we cannot know or control what happens when we encounter difference in the world, we nevertheless have a responsibility when we enter these encounters" (pp. 400–401). As in the earlier encounter, "we are accountable for how we do it: for our attitudes, orientations and capacities in attending to the world and searching for 'truths'" (pp. 400–401).

We also have responsibilities for the effects of encounters. What do we do with blackness, for instance? With the residue and the remains? With the bug, with the ashes of Jayden's burned letter, with the wound to the tree? Yet, these encounters cannot be engaged at the level of principles such as conservation, recycling, or not killing. They require, as van Dooren and Rose (forthcoming) suggest, an "ethics as an openness to others in the material reality of their own lives" (para. 1). They require a becoming-witness.

Davies (2014), drawing on Deleuze, describes *haecceity* as the experience of being immersed in the present moment in such a way that one is acutely affected, completely absorbed, and moved. She writes: "An encounter is an intensity, a becoming that takes you outside of the habitual practices of the already-known, it is intra-active, and corresponds to the power to affect and be affected" (p. 10).

Discussing Dahlberg, she says, "Our capacity to enter into encounters, to re-compose ourselves, to be affected, enhances our specificity, and expands our capacity for thought and action" (p. 1).

Encountering charcoal offered us hope: the hope to be open to thought. The hope to meet anew. The hope to touch and be touched. The hope to attend to anything that came along that wanted attending to. The hope to open ourselves to the unpredictability of the world. The hope, no matter what, to respond to the assemblages we become part of.

4

PAINT

Assemblage

FIGURE 4.1 How does paint invite other materials, and children, to respond?

Sylvia Kind, Author

Anticipate, mix, dab, stab, finger, pat, stir, stroke, flick, color, laugh, compose, orchestrate, impersonate, resound, squish, slip, drip, splatter, mark, slide, blend, merge, bring together, flow, drop, spill, speculate, wrap, arrange, cover, pick up, enact, perform, dance, narrate, improvise, choreograph, modify, spread, massage, pour, caress, exchange, point, exclaim, share, confer, test, immerse, absorb, fill up, fill in, draw out, extend, meander, mingle, empty, combine, converse, scratch, scrub, wipe, wash.

This chapter opens with vibrant tempera paint and is smudged by the strokes of watercolor that drenched our classrooms for months at a time. Educators, researchers, and children encountered paint—a common material in early childhood classrooms—as if we were meeting it for the first time. Instead of asking how the children might experience paint, we asked how paint might choreograph our classrooms. Paint became something to think with rather than a tool to develop toddlers' sensory skills. In this way, paint acted as both verb and noun (Ingold, 2011). Mixing, dipping, stirring, squishing, splattering met anticipation, composition, performance, narration, touch.

Paint blurred distinctions between the child who paints and the painted picture, the blank paper waiting to be covered in paint, the easel standing in the classroom corner, the brushes waiting to be moved by hands, and the plastic bowls holding four brilliant colors of tempera paint. Melting away these boundaries, paint assembled human and nonhuman bodies and became an assemblage in itself.

We noticed paint's viscosity, its ability to dry and solidify, its smoothness, slickness, stickiness. We noticed what paint does—how it spreads, how it covers, how it layers, how it mixes and transforms itself and others, leaving traces behind. Assembling the classroom, paint generated insights, problems, and disruptions for children and educators both. Paint invited bodies to collaborate, to cooperate. It invited forces to interact and interfere with each other. Children, brushes, watercolors, educators, tempera, easels, paper, tables, researchers, walls, and countless other affective bodies came together, both forming each other and breaking apart (Bennett, 2004). Paint assemblages occurred differently at different times and in different spaces in the classroom—gaining or losing force, creating tensions, sometimes stymying, but always forming new orders, new singularities.

In this chapter we trace just a few of these complex interactions among the elements of assemblages formed around paint. An assemblage, Bennett (2010) writes as she borrows from Deleuze and Guattari (1987), is like a "human-nonhuman working group" where each element is in relationship with the others (p. xvii). In the assemblages formed around paint in our classrooms, we were interested in the infinite "*capacities*, rather than the *properties*, of component parts" as well as the "infinite set of other components" (Dittmer, 2013/2014, "Assemblage theory," para.1, emphasis in original) that formed these assemblages. How are paint assemblages transformed? What mixes of forces and intensities emerge in paint assemblages? How does paint open up new potentials for expression and action?

Nothing was determined in these assemblages. Their outcomes were always contingent and open to "the properties and capabilities of non-human components"

(Dittmer, 2013/2014, "Assemblage theory," para. 10). Paint and the other constituent parts of the assemblages we narrate in this chapter "authorise," as Latour (2005a) describes; they "allow, afford, encourage, permit, suggest, influence, block, render possible, forbid, and so on" (p. 72).

Improvising

> *Stained white drop cloths cover the classroom's walls and floor. Tall plexiglass panels in hinged wooden frames zig-zag through the center of the room. On the floor, black plastic bowls of white and purple tempera paint are surrounded by a scattering of paintbrushes. Variations on Rachmaninov's Opus 36 calm the room from a CD player. Leela, barefoot and wearing yellow tights and a blue, maroon, and white striped T-shirt, squats and picks up the bowl of white paint and pours a dollop into the purple paint. Grasping the two nearest paintbrushes, one in each hand, Leela dips the brush ends into the purple paint and quickly stirs in the white. Then she stands and faces the plexiglass.*
>
> *Whoosh, whoosh, whoosh.*
>
> *Leela's arms move up and down in a rapid tandem motion as she colors her plexiglass canvas mauve. Tempera paint's viscidity invites her into a performance. Turning, she looks into the video camera's lens and then stops, stands still, and listens. Raising the paintbrushes into the air, she solemnly conducts the symphony, then turns back toward the plexiglass and strokes in time with the music.*
>
> *Suddenly, Leela drops the paintbrushes onto the floor, squats, and pushes her small hands into white paint, then presses the back of her forearms into the purple paint. Leaning over, she uses her hands to apply white paint to the bottom and top of one foot. Then she raises her foot and drags it across the plexiglass.*
>
> *Bending to the floor, Leela carefully places her left arm into the bowl of white paint and then her right arm into the purple paint. When she stands up straight, the viscous white paint drips slowly down her forearm onto the floor. Holding out her hand, she catches a drip and then smears it onto the plexiglass.*
>
> *Clenching both hands, Leela watches as the paint squishes out between her fingers in long tendrils. The paint is thick, and under force it flows. It is slippery and smooth, so when Leela clenches her fingers around it, it escapes her grasp. Paint is difficult to hold.*

In this classroom ensemble, we are drawn to inventiveness, to extemporization. When tempera entered this toddler classroom, rigid, predictable movements and rules were dispersed like the paint on easels, paper, walls, and bodies. Educators, children, and researchers immersed ourselves in the rhythms and intensities afforded by paint as we opened ourselves to improvisation. "To improvise is to join with the world, or meld with it," Deleuze and Guattari (1987) write, as "one ventures from home on the thread of a tune . . . along sonorous, gestural, motor lines that mark [a] path" (pp. 311–312). This improvisation is not always linear: Lines "graft themselves onto or begin to bud 'lines of drift' with different loops, knots, speeds, movements, gestures and sonorities" (pp. 311–312).

> *In our classroom ensemble, composite bodies such as Leela-paint-concerto-CD-player-plexiglass-purple-paint-and-more-and-more touch each other, and a symphony unfolds.*

Suddenly our developmental early childhood ways to do and be were about, in Stengers' words, *experimenting*—not, as she emphasizes, experimenting *on* or *with* something, which implies "a separation between the experimenter and what she is experimenting on"—but "a practice of active, open, demanding attention to the experience as we experience it" (2008a, p. 109). To say this another way, improvisation and inventiveness, movement and creation became our politics. We could not control the movements of paint, of brushes, of tempera containers on the easel or the table. Momentary encounters with paint exceeded not just us but the paint itself. In the paint assemblages, just as no special place is afforded to the child, no place is reserved for conventional ways of being. In the midst of paint assemblages, we are prompted to ask: What can paint (and child, and brush, and easel) do? What does paint connect to existing assemblages? What new assemblages does paint ignite?

Our curiosity was sparked about what we might do with the intense, often fleeting moments that "happen on the spot, barely noticed and unacknowledged" (Peters, 2009, p. 150), like the preceding one. Deleuze and Guattari (1987) describe such moments as motionless journeys that are "imperceptible, unexpected and subterranean" (p. 148). We quickly became aware that we could not hold on to or control these affective moments—*but we could work with them*. Erin Manning (2007) helped us to make something out of our improvisation, something "which cannot yet be known" (p. xviii). As we came to understand that something not-yet-known is always emerging at the heart of any composition or assemblage, we refocused on the creative potential emerging from paint assemblages: How do brushes, music, paint, Leela, easel, and infinite others form alliances? How do they affect and infect each other? How do they reassemble? How do they hold together and endure? What do these alliances make possible?

Emerging

It is from assemblages' creative potential that form emerges, that bodies become momentarily stable, that something territorializes itself to quickly become undone again, and that the actual is actualized in some form (Deleuze & Guattari, 1987).

An improvisational process "marks and produces the space or territory simultaneously" (Peters, 2009, p. 5). Thus, we paid attention to the ways in which forms emerged in the classroom in paint-easel-child-brush-educator assemblages. In other words, "the processes of composition that produce durable orderings" (Anderson, Kearnes, McFarlane, & Swanton, 2012, p. 175) became our focus, rather than any attempt to bring order and form through structured activities. Always, something different emerged, something that endured in the classroom for weeks and weeks.

Gayle, an educator, is painting with several children near the plexiglass panels. Frankie, Leela, and Saul experiment with painting each other's arms, toes, and cheeks, first with fingers, then with brushes. The paint and the brushes want to play a face-tracing game, so Gayle walks around to the other side of the plexiglass. Kneeling at one of the center panels, she positions her face near the glass and opens her hands, palms out toward the children, who quickly trace around her fingers with their brushes and smear paint across the glass to cloud her face.

Frankie wants a turn having her face traced, so she and Gayle trade places. "Pink, blue, or red?" Gayle asks, and Frankie picks pink. Moving closer to the plexiglass at Gayle's request, Frankie waits expectantly for the paint to be applied to her "face." When Gayle brushes circles around her eyes, she smiles as if feeling snowflakes falling on her skin. Frankie stays perfectly still in anticipation of a move; only her eyes follow the wet brush on the other side of the plexiglass. Pat, pat, pat onto her eyes, mouth, teeth, nose, loose spirals for her hair. "And your chin. I want to tickle your chin!" Arms, hands, fingers. "Do it again!" Frankie shouts. Gayle lightly traces her face again with her brush and Frankie scrambles around to Gayle's side of the plexiglass. "Now your turn!" Gayle lies on her stomach on the floor so that Frankie can easily reach her face. Grasping a brush firmly in her fist, Frankie draws long strokes—down, down—to outline the shape of Gayle's face and then fills in two eyes at the very top of the oval.

A key question for us in paint assemblages like this one was what drives the assemblage forward, opening up new potentials for expression? So often, an interesting aspect of paint assemblages was the importance of repetition. The "doing" of paint—affecting it and being affected by it, even in the simplest case—required sustained activity on the part of the paint-child assemblage. Yet, change and ultimately transformation were essential to embellish, develop, and at times destroy these habitual patterns of activity. Every day, a new element, movement, expression became part of the tracing encounters.

Blending and Bleeding

> *The classroom is alive with color and motion as the children and two educators paint with watercolors at and around a long, low table covered with white paper, brushes, and bright paints. "I'm blending," Eli says as he twirls his brush on the paper, mixing blue and green paint. Above the table, at the bottom of a string suspended from the ceiling, 12-inch strips of paper hang in a bunch, resembling a long-legged spider. Marta and several children are painting the hanging strips. Paint drips and bleeds onto the paint-paper-children-table below.*

As the children and the educators became familiar with paint, they were intensely affected by it. These affections, however, did not occur at an individual or psychological level, as described in Western conventions of developmentally appropriate early childhood education. Affects here are something different. Manning (2010) explains:

> Affect is the transductive force that propels being to become across the phases of its individuation. It is what drives becoming, it is "the liaison between the relation of the individual to itself and the liaison of the individual to the world." Affect is the expression of *a life's* force of becoming in the tight actual-virtual circuit of the preindividual.
>
> *(p. 122, emphasis in original)*

Leaning on Deleuze, O'Sullivan (2006) explains that affect is "the effect a given object of practice has on its beholder, and on its beholder's 'becomings'" (p. 38). Dahlberg and Moss (2009) rely on Massumi's understandings to describe how affect "functions as a sort of contagion that people get involved in, or rather 'hooked on'" (p. xiii). Looking at affect as a transductive force changes the questions in material experimentations from what something is or means to concerns about what the practices set in motion. Affect, in this understanding, is a "break in habit" (O'Sullivan, 2006, p. 22).

Observing the affective atmospheres that would give rise to transformations and transitions in the painting process, we noticed that fairly conventional paint movements and rhythms bled into careful responses to paint's capabilities. Paint capabilities compelled us, children and educators, to try to extend and expand paint assemblages, with varying degrees of success. Paint penetrates even deeper, and blending and bleeding carry on.

> *Long, wide sheets of paper are arranged L-shaped on the wall and floor with a third sheet taped diagonally between them, forming a tent. The children paint various surfaces: the paper on the wall, the top of the tent; others lie on the floor*

underneath and paint the underside. Nearby, Marta sits on the floor reading Eric Carle's "Draw Me a Star" to a small group of children. Taking a cue from Eli's announcement earlier that he was blending the paint, she wants to show him and the other children how the colors in the book's illustrations blend and bleed: the red and orange of the blazing sun, the bright blues, greens, and yellows of the seahorse. "These are watercolors," Marta explains to the children. "You can do a lot of mixing and blending with watercolors." As the story dances along, Marta calls Eli over. "This is the part I especially wanted you to see. What colors did the artist blend to paint the night sky?" "Blue and black!" Eli claps his hands.

Gilbert (2004) suggests that improvising assemblages are most active and capable of expressing themselves when boundaries blur. Watercolors, music, children, fish, book, educators, octopus *become* together as one. The assemblage reaches toward a becoming-paint, a harmonious, resonant, productive flow of intensities moving together in unison. Paint affords the children influence and a presence in the assemblage. The paint assemblage becomes a world of powerful affects and intensities. Here, becoming competent or familiar with paint involves blurring the gap between the manipulations required to use paint in a developmentally focused early childhood classroom and those required in the classroom conditions where this project took place.

Assembling

Two children, Leela and Frankie, and an educator, Mira, are together in front of tall plexiglass panels. Mira, on her knees, paints orange tempera onto the plexiglass with the backs of her hands and forearms while Frankie, sitting cross-legged at the edge of the drop cloth, immerses both her hands in a bowl of peach-colored paint and liberally applies it to her bare feet. Mira extends her hand to Frankie, and as Frankie rubs Mira's forearm with peach paint, Mira massages Frankie's foot. Observing them, Leela decides to take off her shoes, and then massages her right foot with white paint. "Can I rub your foot too?" Mira asks. "No, I will do it," Leela replies matter-of-factly. Frankie scrambles over the bowl of peach paint to sit next to Leela. "Do you want help?" Taking her time to explore the bowl of squishy paint, she coats her small hands with it and then takes Leela's foot between her hands and massages it slowly. The paint is slippery, cool, wet. Reloading her hands with paint, Frankie hovers over Leela's body, considering potential canvases, and then gently presses one hand onto Leela's black pant leg. Next the two girls collaborate to quickly, thoroughly coat Leela's feet, first with white paint, then with orange. Frankie pokes a lone finger into a puddle of white paint on the linoleum. She looks up at Veronica, who is holding the video camera. "Can I paint you, please?" she asks. "Sure, you can paint my hand." Leela joins in and the two girls paint-massage the fingers on Veronica's left hand one by one, then slide their slick hands up her arm. Leela removes excess paint from the back of Veronica's hand and applies it to Veronica's reflection in the plexiglass. Reversing the procedure, she takes paint from the plexiglass and smears it along Veronica's arm. "I'm painting both people," she explains.

Bodies took center stage in our paint assemblages. These bodies, though, were not singular, already-formed canvases of the sensory-input model of developmentally appropriate early childhood practices. Bodies in paint assemblages were always composites in-formation, shift-in-form, creating-with (Manning, 2009). Erin Manning (2009) writes eloquently about these shapeshifting bodies:

> If the body were simply an already formed relegation of organs and sensory input, there would be no potential for recombination. A body as such does not exist—a body *is* not, it *does*. What a body can do depends on its capacity to shape spacetime. Spacetime is shaped according to the movements of a sensing body that cannot yet know what it will mean to sense. To sense is not simply to receive input—it is to invent. Invention springs from open machines of recombination. A body is such a machine, sensing toward infinite recombination. Sense perceptions are not simply "out there" to be analyzed by a static body. They are body-events.
>
> *(p. 212, emphasis in original)*

In paint assemblages, sensing bodies touched each other. In this process of touching, they activated relational movement-toward: they recomposed themselves, moved toward each other, repelled each other, sensed and resensed their proximities, and moved in and out of synchrony. As Manning tells us, touch in paint assemblages was not received, but enacted: "Each touch is much more than a tactile sensory input. It is a hearing-with, a seeing-through" (2009, p. 212). Covering each other with paint is never simply touching someone else's foot. To cover the easel with paint is never to touch a transparent plexiglass. It is an act of worlding; it is, as Manning (2009) explains, "to feel the shapeshifting of spacetime" (p. 212). It is to hear the plexiglass's approach, to express the parameters of the easel expanding and decreasing. It is moving to sense the weight of the brush. It is to move, sensing the wetness of the paint. It is to sense the distance of the easel. It is to recompose the world.

> *The plexiglass panels at the center of the room are covered almost completely with tempera paint. Veronica dabs a paint-loaded sponge to make the glass even more opaque. On the other side, Iniko and Austin hold their breath and wait: They sense Veronica and she senses them. A game of peekaboo erupts and is sustained for two hours. The thick wet paint that covers the plexiglass allows a multiplicity of dialogues. "Can you see me through the paint?" "No." Wipe. "Now I can!" Sponge paint on. "Now I can't." Giggle. Run. Wipe paint off, sponge it on. "Can you see me now?" Wiping one tiny hole in the paint reveals the other. Sponges in hand, the painters become plexiglass-Austin-wet-squishy-paint-Veronica-laughter-Iniko-running-smearing-squealing-sensing-bodies.*

What takes place in these paint assemblages is more than what happens in the child's mind or brain. These assemblages are about worlding, as we discovered earlier. Drawing on philosopher Whitehead, Manning (2009) writes about the difference between sense-data produced in the brain and in the world: "Refuting the simplistic notion of stimuli-response that is always based on a subject in a pre-formed world," Whitehead prefers "to think of the body-world as processual . . . as a technique for recomposition" where "the senses can no longer be thought as external stimuli pre-composed for integration into the subjective life of a biological body" (p. 218). Sensing bodies do not yet know what it will mean to sense. As Manning writes, "bodies, senses, and worlds recombine to create new events" (p. 218).

New events, new connections, new sensations emerged in paint assemblages.

Creating

Paint assemblages garner momentum. They are uncontained. They depend on their creative force. Paint assemblages act as affirmative creations, and affirmative creation, as Manning sees it, is about creating more life. It is about worlding a world and composing-with. It is becoming with "the force of *a life*" (Manning, 2010, p. 171, emphasis in original). Paint assemblages are alive. They have a life of their own that it is more than the sum of their parts. They follow life.

> *Frankie and Leela are exuberant today. Perhaps it's because of the sun streaming in through the studio's large windows. They want to balance, march, dance, take their shoes off, sing, dance some more. They collect the large sheets of paper that have covered the walls and the easel for the last few days. The papers have absorbed bright tempera colors, suggesting costumes. The two girls chase each other around*

> *a double easel. Each has her own sheet of clean white paper. Frankie covers every inch of hers with red paint. Brush, brush, brush, she paints her hands red and holds them out, squealing, "Reddy, reddy!" Soon Leela's hands and arms are also red. Joining their crimson hands together, they cavort in a circle, as the room and the paper and the paint come alive. Collapse, jump up, start over again.*

Paint assemblages are agitated, stirred in their relations. Yet not everything goes. Paint assemblages could fade away or take a wrong turn. Thus, sustaining relations and bodies' capacities to affect and be affected becomes crucial.

It is in these relations that the ethos of paint assemblages lies. Manning (2010) writes:

> An ethics of relation is an act that agitates at the level of thought-feeling, in the event: an ethics of relation has concern for the event in its emergence, refuting knower/known hierarchies, preferring instead a horizontalizing milieu of experience where what emerges conditions the stakes of its coming-to-be.
>
> *(p. 171)*

What concerns us as educators and researchers are relations: the dynamic relations between and across various elements, such as purple paint, child, red paint, us, watercolors, music, brushes, sun streaming through the window, and plexiglass, to name but a few. Zylinska (2014) refers to these relations as minimal ethics, or an ethics of life. For us, it is a minimal pedagogy: nonsystemic, nonhubristic, and nonnormative. Nothing to reproduce. Always open to creation. Always sustaining the relations and ecologies of emerging assemblages.

5
CLAY
Ecologies

FIGURE 5.1 We want to discover how clay acts and interacts in ecologies

Sylvia Kind, Author

Pinch it, poke it, press it, shape it, throw it, scrape it, form it, lift it. Clay is incredibly versatile. It can be sliced, engraved, embellished, glazed, washed, carried, burnished, heaved, fired, dropped, shaped, sculpted, soaked, sprayed, hollowed, altered, polished, painted, pounded, flattened, carved, transformed. Clay moves, wobbles, weeps, sticks, shrinks, dries, extends, gestures, melts, trickles, sits, tears, breaks, collapses, rises, attaches, shudders, rests, accumulates.

This chapter engages with the problems clay poses and, more precisely, with its demands. Clay makes plenty of demands. When it is fired, for example, it demands extreme care. If it cools too quickly, it is prone to dunt. If its naturally occurring carbon doesn't burn in just the right way, the object's core might blacken or bloat. Air pockets known as blebs, which form when the clay is shaped, might blister or pit the object's glaze. If clay's particles become ionized and repel each other, clay might liquefy and become unworkable. Once clay is dry and hard, it shrinks. When it cracks, it returns to dust. Once dust, it can be collected and soaked again—but not if stirred.

In this chapter we describe three "clay ecologies" where children and educators worked together with clay: in an atrium studio in an early childhood center, at a river, and in a forest. In these three ecologies, we encountered clay as "a site of invention" (Stengers, Manning, & Massumi, 2009, p. 3) where the pragmatics of our questions were "much more alive, more vivid, more difficult to forget" (p. 3) than any truth about clay.

One of many things we learned in our atrium, river, and forest studios is that clay ecologies force educators and children to think. To hesitate. To feel. To notice. To question. These ecologies demand close attention, nourishment, and situated competencies. They remind us that not everything is a human construction, that there is no norm, and that each piece of clay acts differently.

Clay in the Atrium Studio

The studio is a large, bright atrium in the early childhood center, with hallways and rooms opening onto it. A large canvas drop cloth splotched with bright paint carpets the linoleum, and a low, white modular table is positioned at the hub. On it are several pruned tree branches and a multitude of rocks, pebbles, and pieces of clay in varying shapes and sizes: ovoids, chunks, balls, disks. The table has a drawer at one end that is ideal for stashing rocks, clay, and twigs.

Like a pop-up art gallery, the atrium studio isn't permanent. The space is re-created as a clay ecology every Tuesday. Like any studio, the atrium is a place for thinking, doing, feeling, and testing out materials. It allows us to focus creatively on an idea or a problem. It offers a place to work together to produce something, whether it be a sculpture, a performance, or documented work.

Unlike the cool, damp forest and river studios, which help keep the clay soft and squishy, the atrium is warm and dry, and the clay hardens fast.

Working in the atrium draws our attention to comings and goings, to people passing through, to the clock on the wall, to the flicker of fluorescent light above our heads. To objects brought here from somewhere else: fragments of tree branch, stones, clay, pebbles, bits of fir-needled stem. Children's bodies come and go through the atrium. Hand after hand after hand and a multitude of feet touch the same piece of clay, warming it and cooling it, shaping it, pounding it, changing it.

Clay in the Forest

We created the forest clay studio in a small wood near the early childhood center. A creek bed that fills with water in wet weather runs through it. Clay in the forest invites different movements than those we see in the atrium. Here we are keenly aware of being entangled in the midst of relationships among the ground, trees, water, birds, deer, us, plants, insects, pine needles, clay. Transformations abound through the process of working with clay: Clay adheres to branches, disappears when immersed in water, and rolls through the forest humus picking up its leaf litter. The children transform the forest and the forest changes the children. Connections are made. Some are expected: clay–sticks; clay–water; hands–clay; forest–jump; jump–run. Some we did not expect: clay–boots; trees–children; forest–worm; raven–call. Others are both surprising and endearing: a deer approaches the studio and quietly observes our movements with clay; a spider living in a hollow tree stays still as the children press clay around its web; a woodpecker feasts on bugs in a tree high above us. Clay becomes a multispecies event.

So much catches our attention as we encounter clay in the forest. Some of us focus on marks and tracks left by sticks, rocks, animals, water, people, fallen leaves on the clay. Some of us pay attention to the clay's color, its smell, its texture and malleability. For others, working with clay in the forest draws our attention to the land we are standing on and living in. We pay attention to how we might think with children about the ongoing settler occupation of this land. We pay attention to the land that was disrupted so that clay could be manufactured for the purpose of making art.

Clay at the River

The river basin is wide, but the river is low, so our studio is a broad sea of fallen leaves and round stones—stones that are hard for children's rubber-boot-clad feet to walk on, stones that invite small hands to pick them up to inspect them, throw them, build with them, slip them into pockets, carry them home. Clap two rocks together, slide a chunk of clay between them, press a leaf into the surface of the clay. A large rock turns into a workbench, a small one into a hammer to pound wet clay into submission. Hands shape slippery, squishy clay into a bowl to scoop cold water from the river to drink. We and the children navigate the sea of stones to extract ancient clay from the river basin, to "wash" it in water, to press it against our skin and hold it in our hands. The clay melts back into the river and disappears.

Working with clay at the river draws our attention to how clay feels in our hands when we touch it, when we drape it over stones and smooth it, when it's cold, when it's wet, when it squeezes through our fingers, when we punch it with our hands, when we push it like a sponge to scrub granite.

Working with clay at the river draws our attention to water.

Meso and Ethoecology

To think about clay ecologies, we draw from Isabelle Stengers' concept of the milieu (Stengers et al., 2009), which allows us to pay attention to clay's specificities. Clay demands something different in each distinct and equally dynamic ecology. The concept of ecology enfolds the radical specificity of clay and its capacities. It enables us not only to work with clay in its milieu, but to think about clay's relation with a milieu.

Clay acts/demands/lives differently in the atrium, river, and forest, thus each clay ecology "obliges us to think through the 'middle,' through the milieu" (Stengers et al., 2009, p. 4). Stengers refers to this middle as "the meso" (p. 3), and says:

> The idea of the "meso" is quite new. . . . Microphysics is well known, it's the stuff of physicists' dreams. The macro in physics is also familiar, it's crystals, liquids, and bodies that can be characterized by general, measurable properties. But the meso is neither of these. It concerns not matter, but material. Why does glue stick? Why do metals tend to stress and break? This is a science of the interstices and the cracks. It's a science of defects. It is the kind of science where it is always a question of *this* material, rather than Matter.
>
> *(p. 3, emphasis in original)*

Rather than inviting us to think about the child's micro and macro contexts and ask questions that focus on what happens in children's contexts, as Bronfenbrenner (1979) would, the idea of the meso takes us somewhere else.

The meso necessitates what Stengers calls an *ethoecology*, "where the *ethos* of the molecule [in this case, molecules of clay], that which it is capable of, cannot be dissociated from its *oikos*, from the milieu requiring this ethos" (Stengers et al., 2009, p. 3). Ethoecologies—including our clay ecologies—demand "delocalized interactions" that resist totality (Stengers et al., 2009, p. 3). Stengers, a chemist-philosopher, is talking here about chemistry, where to be delocalized is to be shared among more than two atoms in a molecule. Ethoecologies, for Stengers, are about connection, and connection "is a matter of 'coming into existence' which demands both trust and an art of immanent discrimination" (Stengers, 2008b, p. 39). The questions to ask, Stengers suggests, must be specific and bring "characters into existence" (Stengers et al., 2009, p. 3). For example:

> What is a crack? How does this propagate? How is that encountered? What brings this to a threshold, where it breaks? These are questions which demand the invention of beings, such as the crack, that are called for with a manner of being all their own, and which enter more into narratives than into deductions.
>
> *(Stengers et al., 2009, p. 3)*

Inspired by Stengers, we began to question clay's specificity: Why does clay adhere so well to a tree on a rainy morning? Why do dry pine needles stick so easily to clay? Why does clay tend to crack in the sun? Why must clay be touched with warm hands to become more pliable? Why is it impossible to work with clay when wearing mittens on a cold morning? Why does this river carry remnants of clay that leave traces on the bluish rocks?

Going deeper, we asked: What does this clay ecology demand from us? Does it demand betrayal, does it "mak[e] perceptible the possibility of a jump we can and may make? Or is it demanding surrender—surrendering our own attachments in the name of a demand that would then transcend them" (Stengers, 2008b, p. 45)?

These questions led us to surrender our attachments to attachment theory.

Attachments

In the forest clay ecology, moss attaches to cedar tree, and clay attaches to moss. Bark oozes "yucky" sap and clay presses down, hiding the sap through its attachment. Pine needles jump onto clay that is dropped on the ground; they attach of their own accord. Clay helps us see connections. Pine needles, sticks, rocks, moss, soil, leaves, twigs, fingers, garbage stick to clay. Clay transforms itself over and over as it comes into friction with things, and with us. Clay never stays the same. It collects things. It morphs. Its attachments transform it, and us.

Attachments here are different from the developmental attachments of children to adults and more-than-humans that are common knowledge in early childhood education (see Ainsworth, 1969; Bowlby, 1969, 1973, 1980). Attachments in clay ecologies are the attachments of children to the repeated task of pressing clay onto tree trunks, the poetry of molding wet clay, the interdependence of children and trees, the entanglements of clay, bark, and moss, the mutualism of river and clay, the parasitism of English ivy on the cedar tree where the clay adheres.

Attachments involve the interactions that create and sustain these clay ecologies. These attachments have a political undertone, as Stengers proposes: They counter capitalism. Current modes of capital work against, undo, and destroy attachments. For instance, attachments to land have shifted now that land is viewed less as a source of sustenance and more as a resource to be exploited. In Stengers' view, we might be able to refigure our attachments through the meso; she says: "The . . . success of a meso device would be to confer upon a situation the power to make those who are attached to it . . . think together. Not overcome the conflict, but transversalize its terms" (Stengers et al., 2009, p. 5). We attach to these encounters with clay hoping to throw into question the terms and conditions of capitalist practices. What attachment practices might emerge from clay ecologies? What attachment practices might be renegotiated through these clay ecologies?

As we work with clay and clay works with us in the forest and at the river, we ourselves are thrown into question. Clay ecologies demand that we think and feel coevolution, parasitism, autopoiesis, symbiosis, interdependence, mutualism, mimicry, predation, extinction, resilience, metabolism, and other concepts that reattach us to clay. How might clay practices be thought ecologically? How might ecological thinking be practiced in early childhood education? How might clay ecologies relate, entangle, interlink to world making, sense making, change making? These are never generalized questions. An attachment is an event, as Stengers asserts, "which cannot be discussed at the level of its general conditions. You don't mimic attachments, and you can't replace them with collaborationist good will" (Stengers et al., 2009, p. 5).

> *Kiri scoops clay from the river in a lump and shapes it, so very carefully, into a bowl, turning, molding, moistening with small fingers, attaching to the clay, to the water, to the stones she is squatting on. At last her bowl is ready to be dipped into the river and filled with clear, cold water: clay reattaching to the river, clay and water and hands and air entangled.*

It Matters

Donna Haraway (2015), inspired by the thinking of Marilyn Strathern and others, has been reminding us since the early 1990s that "it matters what stories tell stories, it matters what thoughts think thoughts, it matters what worlds world worlds" (para. 7). Working in *this* forest with this specific lump of clay matters. Feeling this piece of clay and pushing it into this broken tree matters. It is not just a random lump of clay in a random forest near a random river. It matters where the clay goes, what this particular ball of clay affords in this specific tree.

> *Rianna stands in the forest holding a small lump of clay in her hands. Looking around, she carefully selects a tree to receive the clay. It matters which tree the clay attaches to. This tree is broken; it is dead. It is a stump, its trunk sawn off clean by some long-ago blade. The stump's flesh is hard and dry, its bark still ridged. Rianna presses the clay with all her might. Attaching takes work. Back and forth she runs to find more clay, and then attaches each small piece, clay onto clay, building up a good-sized mound. It matters how she moves the clay, how she moves her body. Sometimes, instead of running, she drops to the ground and rolls, up the hill and down, to find more clay. Quickly, knees tucked in, then slowly, feet waving at the sky, she rolls her story of attaching clay to tree.*

The clay in the forest and the clay in the river need to be taken seriously because each demands different kinds of emotional, intellectual, and material skills (Haraway, 2015). Clay tells other stories in the forest than the ones it tells at the river, which are different again from the stories it tells in the atrium. Clay on trees tells a different story than clay on rocks. Clay destabilizes stories in the forest, river, and atrium. Clay on sticks retells the stories of clay on trees, and vice versa. To put it in Haraway's terms, clay ecologies hold "a kind of serious denormalization of that which is normally held still, in order to do that which one thinks one is doing" (para. 7). And it matters, she says, "to destabilize worlds of thinking with other worlds of thinking. It matters to be less parochial" (para. 7).

> *In the forest, as at the river, as in the atrium, the children's clay attachments are carefully crafted. Some are balls. Some are snakes. Some are pancakes, flat and lumpy. Some are pressed onto an ancient living cedar, others onto stumps. It matters which shape attaches to which tree.*

Fostering and Nourishing

Clay is soil, and soil requires fostering and nourishment. When we extract clay from the river, when we offer it to children, we are to do it with care. We are to fashion, paraphrasing Maria Puig de la Bellacasa (2015), modes of clay care.

These modes of care recognize that clay is more than an art commodity for children's use. Clay care requires thinking from the perspective of maintaining a web of relations "involved in the very possibility of" ecologies, rather than thinking only of their potential benefits to children (p. 701). Clay is living, because it holds potential "to transform relations of care" (p. 703). Clay soil is a multispecies community (p. 701).

Neeta, Carly, and the other children shape marshmallows out of clay and poke them onto the ends of sticks to roast them over a clay-and-stick fire. Carly's is an acorn-marshmallow. She smooths and pats and pinches the clay on the end of her knobby stick. Neeta squeals when her marshmallow "catches fire." Holding it close to her lips, she quickly blows on it before it can burn.

Perhaps Neeta and Carly's vivid adventure of roasting clay marshmallows can be connected to the idea of caring for clay differently. Marshmallows are attended to meticulously, with each connection cared for: stick and marshmallow cared for, marshmallow and fire, fire and sticks. It might be an act of fabricating a line of flight (Deleuze & Guattari, 1987), a line that, in Stengers' words, "does not denounce, but rather betrays, makes perceptible the special power of the territory" (2008b, p. 39). To betray "is always a matter of encounter and connection" (p. 39), Stengers says, disclosing "an ingredient that both belongs to the territory and connects with an outside against which this territory protects itself" (p. 42). Betraying clay as a material of consumption, Neeta and Carly "dared to propose that we were not prisoners of those categories" (p. 51). Clay is not clay anymore. Clay is a marshmallow. An acorn–marshmallow. Fire. Naming clay as clay would mean sliding back to the usual understandings of clay, to stratifications of clay that make us forget that we can indeed care for clay differently. Perhaps seeing Neeta and Carly's clay marshmallows as betrayals can help us create new linkages. Spaces of betrayal, Stengers (2007) reminds us,

> are to be made, linkage by linkage, step by step. The joy of productive connexions cannot be betrayed, it will proceed as it must, and needs no model, no master thinker. It does not need the togetherness of a mobilized group against an enemy, what it produces is rather a wild bunch, with diverging singular paths resonating with each other, each becoming more apt to resist because of the delocalized co-presence of others. It cannot be confused with the global law of the market plus a principle of freedom meaning that everyone can grab whatever [they feel] like.
>
> *(para. 39)*

In an age of brutal capitalism (Stengers, 2015), the practices of joyful linking, of caring and building connections for a different world are crucial. Care, for the most part, has itself been appropriated in early childhood education, rendering work with young children an affective labor integral to the capitalist apparatus (Hodgins, 2014). But what if there were an alternative? Neeta and Carly's caring act of roasting clay marshmallows renders a revolutionary approach to caring that is adequate to the challenges these children face in their lived engagements with the world (Taylor & Pacini-Ketchabaw, 2015). This act tells us educators and researchers that there is more in the world than capital modes of production. Roasting clay marshmallows allows for the production of new subjectivities, relationships, and social configurations.

Folding in

Tara, an educator, sits on the ground beside the creek in the forest studio and manipulates a small lump of clay. A group of children gathered around hand her objects to fold into the clay: sappy needles, bits of lichen, rocks, twigs, more clay. "What shall we do with these?" Tara asks. "Squish them!" Tara thumbs a hole in the center of the clay to accept the children's offerings. The push creates an unexpected sculpture: a bowl that contains and hides the objects the children had stuck to the clay. Tilting their heads close, the children and Tara listen to the whispers of the rocks and the pine needles hiding in the bowl. More clay, more objects are folded in, and the lump grows bigger. Tara carries it to the creek and smooths it with water, sealing everything in, for now.

Stengers refers to folding as "something like a history . . . which obliges us to think through the 'middle,' through the milieu" (Stengers et al., 2009, p. 3). As with the bowl the children and Tara are shaping, experiences, feelings, memories, and histories are constantly folded in. Not just those of the children, but those of the clay, the rocks, the pine needles, and the racing waters of the creek.

The concept of folding helps us avoid binaries in our thinking: There are not splits into two, says Stengers (cited in Latour, 2005b, p. 227), but folds. There is always a continuation that takes place through folding. We fold in an experience. The clay folds in pine needles. We fold in the memory of a dry pine needle attaching itself to cold clay. The clay folds in the touch of our warm hand. We fold in the smooth sensation of the wet clay. And so on. Bruno Latour (2005b), writing about Stengers' work, refers to the idea of the fold as bearing witness, as continuation of a life, where children endure in their existence, where clay endures in its existence, where we endure in our existence. It is the fold that "forces those it rallies to think, imagine, create" (Stengers et al., 2009, para. 7).

> *For three months, Tara and the children fold stories, sounds, ideas into the clay. They wonder together: What might the clay be able to hold? As it turns out, clay holds much: twigs, tears, moss, wishes, the memory of a distant raven's call, squeals of laughter, crisp spring air, disappointment, paper, questions, exuberance, reluctance, warmth, water, seeds.*

Ecologies of Practice

> *Andra, a dance instructor, has come to the atrium to dance with the children. A large canvas drop sheet is spread out across the linoleum, scattered with balls of clay and cookie sheets filled with large and small chunks of ice. Together, Andra and the children and the ice and the clay will choreograph a dance. First the children and Andra warm up their bodies. Sitting on the floor, they are thinking together with the ice and the clay: smooth and slow, fast and sharp. Stretching, stroking, clapping, reaching, flexing. Then they rise and move: slow, fast, wriggle, stretch, shake, stealthy, smooth, spin, jump, balance, flow. Music joins in: quick, exciting, drumbeat, circle, spinning, rolling.*
>
> *Everyone and everything joins in the dance. Ice presses into clay; feet pound clay smooth; bodies jump; ice melts; bodies roll; clay sweats: slick, cool, hard balls, slippery, wet. Clay coats hands, arms, fingers, slides between toes. Ice drips, melts, pools. Drum beats, rhythm, bodies move: slowly, faster, faster, march, spin, fall.*

Drawing on Pickering, Stengers (2008a) speaks of "a dance of agency" in ecologies of practice, "with the practitioner tentatively constructing a device, then adopting a passive role in order to follow the consequences of its functioning, then intervening again" (p. 97). She argues that "the problem for each practice is how to foster its own force, make present what causes practitioners to think and feel and act" (Stengers, 2005, p. 195). A dance of agency is performed by the children and the clay and the ice and the drum.

Each achievement in this clay-child-ice-drum-dance ecology is always a partial relation, "a mutation which does not depend on humans only, but on humans as belonging" to an ecology in which children "are obliged and exposed by their obligations" (Stengers, 2005, p. 192). It is a dance of fostering relations. It is a challenging dance. To foster these relations, children are to take the stance that, as Stengers puts it, they "are not alone in the world" (p. 192).

The dance emerged only after many months of fostering relationships with clay. Before it could emerge, we had to understand what clay makes possible. We had to feel what clay is capable of. We had to listen to clay's demands, work with clay's problems, and work against them.

As the children dance, the warmth of the room melts the ice. Slick blobs and puddles of melted clay and ice dot the canvas. These puddles offer themselves as rinks for the children to skate across, their movements barely controlled. Azizi slips and falls to the ground, scrambles up, and keeps dancing to the beat of the drum.

The responses of clay and child are never predictable, because ecologies of practice are always emergent. Movements are not intentionally performed: They emerge. Clay responds to children's movements as they work with it. Yet, sometimes it resists and refuses to stay still in one shape. It is impossible, though, to predict these resistances. Clay flows through the studio in rhythm with the children's movements. It demands transformation through its easy malleability and flexibility. Clay is able to slow things down in the studio. It invites the children to follow its unexpected movements as it interacts with shoes, with pockets, with canvas, with floor, with hands, with mittens, with air. In the dance-clay ecology, the production that is going on has a life of its own.

6
BLOCKS

Time

FIGURE 6.1 What does paying attention to blocks in interaction with other things set in motion?

Sylvia Kind, Author

Stack, clack, whack, topple, knock, look, gather, fall, collect, sort, evaluate, hide, conceal, watch, construct, offer, push, glide, ride, transport, run, chase, borrow, use, deplete, find, guard, intensify, accelerate, approach, desire, assemble, loosen, keep, enclose, extend, tear down, build up, pull out, observe, measure, dismantle, encircle, regulate, fabricate, improvise, reorganize, consider, gaze, glance, balance, pause, seek, plan, stand on, sit beside, happen upon, reconstruct, release, retreat, restart. Wooden blocks are solid. They are dense. They have a shape. They cannot be ground up, crunched, or torn.

The early childhood center purchased a new set of wooden blocks, which allowed us to begin at the beginning with blocks. Together with the children we struggled to unpick the clear packing tape, removed the crumpled balls of newsprint from the box, and extracted, one by one, the carefully arranged smooth, glossy, beautiful, precision-cut blocks.

Of course, the blocks began long before they came to us. Decades or even centuries before we met them, they had been seeds that grew into particular trees in a particular place. Much later, they were cut by particular saw blades and shipped on flatbed trucks to a mill, milled by millwrights, shipped again, manufactured as blocks on an assembly line, packaged, and shipped to the educational supply center that sent them to us by delivery truck.

The histories and geographies of these particular blocks became almost an obsession for us: When were these blocks made? When and where were the boxes the blocks were packed into made? What kind of wood were the blocks made from? In what forest did the trees they were made from grow? How long did it take to make the trees into blocks? How long did it take for the blocks to arrive to us after the trees were cut? How old were the trees that were sliced into pieces to craft our shiny new blocks? These and many more questions provoked us to trace these blocks' histories and geographies and consequently to attend to blocks in unexpected ways.

Time quickly became an important element in the project. Time is layered. Bodied memories of carrying heavy blocks and methodically building roads intertwine with histories of the material, the present, and the future. Entanglements of the past, the future, and the now exist as children move in the classroom around the blocks, carrying with them blocks' structured qualities. How do we see these complex time-spaces in between?

We tend to link time to predictable, measurable, regulated movement or change. In early childhood education classrooms, time is perceived as linear, extensive (Kummen, 2010; Pacini-Ketchabaw, 2012, 2013; Rose & Whitty, 2010; Wien, 1996). It comprises identical units. Encountering blocks, attending to their flows and enclosures and tracing their connections to multiple localities and globalities led us to question our tendency to emphasize "clock time": What if time encompasses more than static movements? If moments are not linear, if they do not end, might they flow with our bodies?

In this chapter, we join many theorists and artists (e.g., Barad, 2007; Bergson, 1991; Casarino, 2003; Colebrook, 2002; Coleman, 2008, 2009; Deleuze, 2006; Grosz, 1999a, 1999b, 2005a, 2005b; Ingold, 2011; Oates, n.d.; Wolseley, 2009/2010, 2016) to question time's epistemic, ontological, political status as we build complex structures with blocks. We map how time is not a neutral medium in which life can be framed or matter constructed. With blocks, we think of time as an active, dynamic participant in framing life. Time—as unpredictable, a materializing force that innovates and surprises—is the focus of this chapter.

The Weight of Time

We set aside three months for the block exploration and moved to a large, empty (adult) classroom beside the studio so we could explore without needing to tidy away at day's end. The room's large, bright windows overlooked a quiet roadway next to a forest of fir and cedar trees. We removed the classroom tables and stacked the chairs at one end of the room to give ourselves lots of room to spread out, to make room for possibilities for the blocks to become many things, for the children to use the blocks in any way they chose. We hoped for open, divergent explorations without the usual limits we encounter in the center.

No one, teachers included, said anything about how blocks could or should be used, but it quickly became evident that block-building "rules" did exist. The rules emerged in interaction: blocks are for building and making things; once you build something, no one else can take it apart; once something is constructed, it stays there, and only the builder—or those whom the builder chooses—can decide how to rearrange the blocks. We notice right away how static and stable blocks appear.

With the blocks we felt the weight of history in the room. Like growth rings on a tree, wooden blocks carry traces of times past that made our experimentations stutter.

Early childhood education historian Larry Prochner (2011) traces the history of blocks in North America. He links the emergence of blocks to Froebel's famous gifts, but he also notes the importance of German manufacturer Milton Bradley, which has manufactured blocks since the 1870s, to our current practices of block construction. Producing many different kinds of blocks (gifts; precisely cut; cheaper, imperfectly cut blocks; unboxed sets of regular-quality blocks, similar to bricks), Bradley marked every early childhood classroom. Prochner writes:

FIGURE 6.2 Bradley's Kindergarten Alphabet Building Blocks
© The Strong

"Although blocks changed in form, becoming larger, the pedagogy proved durable" (p. 375).

Prochner (2011) writes:

> Blocks were sold in "neat, strong, varnished cherry boxes" for storage and presentation according to a ritual derived from Froebel. Even the six knitted balls that comprised gift 1 came in a wooden box. Individual blocks were made from maple to eliminate warping and were unpainted and unadorned. Blocks needed to be cut precisely to enable children to make complex structures. The company highlighted the high-quality construction of its product; there was nothing else to distinguish it from the product of its competitors. A catalogue from the 1880s quoted an unnamed "leading kindergartner" as stating that the equipment "is simply perfect, so far as human eyes and fingers are concerned." Nevertheless, "for those wishing cheaper goods" the company also sold imperfectly cut blocks without labels or a guarantee.
>
> *(p. 361)*

Blocks have always been heavy with expectation. At the time of their emergence, blocks were marketed as a way to "improve the quality of children's output and increased the efficiency of their learning" (Prochner, 2011, p. 363). Today educators look to block play to develop children's creativity and imagination (Honegger, n.d.). Blocks are governed by "rules" and come weighted with instructions. There are stages for block building, guidelines for how educators are to scaffold during block play, suggestions for what materials to add to the block play area, and examples of vocabulary that needs to be introduced and reinforced during block play.

> *Our bodies become distanced from the intense intra-actions in the studio with paper, clay, paint, and charcoal, yet the force of time continues to move with our bodies. As we become aware of the weight of blocks' expectations, we want to chop up, saw, and reduce some of the blocks to sawdust, but the expense of the blocks, the perfection of their milling and measurement, and the expectation of what blocks are meant to do for children stop us in our tracks. We want to think differently about blocks, but everything seems to confirm that a "block is a block, is a block, is a block." We imagine bringing in a wood plane or a chipper to reimagine the bricks' form. We think about nails and hammers, but we wonder what other educators would think or say if they saw the beautiful, expensive new blocks chopped up or nailed together. We find ourselves stumped.*

What can we do with a block that won't fly and can't change its shape? We teachers felt the need to experiment, too. We bristled at being limited by the weight of history and the block-building rules. It seems that in the block events, at least until more materials joined in the explorations, we were constantly working to provoke, to open up spaces, and to keep things in movement. But blocks stopped us.

We began to question our own actions—do we approach things as if they are always new, wiping away the reminders of the previous day's play, taking down structures, putting the blocks away, creating "new" invitations? Do materials hold memory? And if so, how? It seems that blocks carry traces of inherited histories, meanings, and "appropriate" actions. Could this weight of time invite new memories? How do we live with the rhythm of these moments of intensity throughout the day? How can we play with time?

Playing With Time

Australian artist John Wolseley (2016) plays with the idea of time in his work. In his paintings of a place, Wolseley brings together the histories and stories of three different times: deep time, shallow time, and now time. Deep time is the time of the earth, the time of geology. This time is about timeliness. Shallow time is the time created through the ongoing process of European colonization. Perhaps we can link shallow time with clock time. Now time is the time at which Wolseley paints his pictures. In his natural history of a swamp, Wolseley (2009/2010) eloquently speaks about playing with time:

> I like the idea that a given swamp or wetland contains within it. The history of the world. As I paint these wetlands a sense of this history loomed in the back of my mind. A history of deep time which has been so beautifully revealed in the Vostok Core. This core of ice, several kilometres deep, is a vertical record of the changing conditions of the earth's climate laid down over 400,000 years. Here one can "read," the periods of hot and cold, and the glacial and interglacial times; and one can also see repeated at intervals the great swampy times such as in the Carboniferous and Permian periods when much of the world was damp and marshy. The cycles of Deep Time of dry/wet, desert/swamp are all there as rhythmic as a heartbeat. One gets a sense of how these conditions repeat themselves in a cycle of eternal return.
>
> *(Movement 4: Swamp, para. 2)*

We continue to play with blocks and begin to play with time. We try knitting covers for some of the blocks to soften their form, but this doesn't change things much. We discover some red and blue cardboard blocks in the cupboard. They are similar in size to the largest wooden blocks, but much lighter. We cover them with papier-mâché newspaper strips and the children play with them as a puzzle. They are carried around, turned over and over, thrown, their corners picked at. "What are they? Can I open them? Unwrap them? Are they presents? What can I do with them?" The papier-mâché blocks travel between the paper explorations and the block events, sometimes back and forth. We notice that, while the precisely cut geometric wooden blocks tended to be steady and slow, weighted by particular histories and rules of behavior, the papier-mâché blocks along with sticks and driftwood pieces moved freely, often wildly, running about with the children, being transformed and put to many uses, easily exchanged by children and across spaces in the room. The wooden blocks, in contrast, once the children had used them in a construction, tended to stay in place, as if frozen in time.

Block play in early childhood education practice rests on a dominant idea of time that is characteristic of Western thought: time as "spatialized" by having been divided into discrete units (Casarino, 2003). Colebrook (2002) explains that

> we tend to think of time as the connection of homogeneous or equivalent units within some already given whole; we think of a world in which

there is time, or a world that then goes through time. We put being before becoming. We imagine time as a series of "nows."

(p. 41)

Just as the blocks have a history, so does clock time. Here is how Michel Foucault (1977) describes the presence of clocks in 19th-century classrooms:

At the last stroke of the hour, a pupil will ring the bell, and at the first sound of the bell all the pupils will kneel, with their arms crossed and their eyes lowered. When the prayer has been said, the teacher will strike the signal once to indicate that the pupils should get up, a second time as a signal that they should salute Christ, and a third that they should sit down.

(p. 150)

The first European clocks alerted monks in monasteries when it was time for their regular prayers (Boorstin, 1983). Later, clocks were considered as "not only a device of immediate practical utility but also an investment in the future" (Sawhney, 2004, p. 372). The clock emerged with and participated in batch production, the use of interchangeable parts, tooth- and wheel-cutting machines, and advances in manufacturing (Sawhney, 2004). The clock enabled the synchronization of local and regional commerce (Sawhney, 2004). Interacting with the telegraph, the clock afforded the emergence of standard time in the late 1800s. Carey (1989) describes this momentous event: "When it reached one o'clock over the center of the Eastern time zone, the clocks were stopped at noon in Chicago and held for nine minutes and thirty-two seconds until the sun centered on the 90th meridian" (p. 226). Clocks also afforded the conditions for moral rules of conduct. Levine, for instance, quotes the following statement from a catalog published by the Electric Signal Clock Company in 1891: "If there is one virtue that should be cultivated more than any other by him who would succeed in life, it is punctuality; if there is one error to be avoided, it is being behind time" (Levine, 1998, p. 67).

The clock plays a prominent role in early childhood practices. Kummen (2010), Rose and Whitty (2010), Wien (1996), and Wien and Kirby-Smith (1998) have analyzed the tyranny of time: the clock shaping educators' practices and regulating children's schedules; time dominating daily practices; clocks creating a frenzy in the classroom; children moving efficiently through clock time; educators running to be on time. With the clock, structures become solidified. We wondered: What kinds of work does the clock do? What role do humans play in operating and producing clocking practices? What role does the clock play in producing early childhood practices and in reconfiguring human–clock boundaries and relations? What sort of temporalities do different clocking practices engender? What sort of shifts in assemblages do different clocks and different clocking practices encourage? How are specific practices of early childhood education mediated by various clocks and clocking practices? Do different clocks in different spaces do different work and engender different bodies/bodily practices and relations?

After the initial unpacking of the blocks and the first constructions, the children begin to comment that all the blocks are being used up. By the end of the second morning, all of the blocks have been used in different constructions and arrangements, and the children speculate about bringing in more blocks from their classroom so they can keep building. We decide to play with this problem through exaggerating the "using up" and the static nature of the blocks. Before the next event, we gather all the blocks in the center of the room and build one large structure, enclosing interesting materials such as small toys, sticks, hearts, and plasticine inside the main tower so that the children would have to remove some blocks to take these items out.

When the children enter the room, they greet this structure by pointing, questioning, walking toward it, inspecting it, and encircling it with running games. No one touches it at first, but soon loose hearts and plasticine are carefully drawn out and collected. Smaller blocks are removed, held, and replaced. A few unconventional pieces, such as curved wooden blocks that don't seem connected to the rest, are taken away. Long paper tubes and sticks trapped in the middle are retrieved and transformed into hockey sticks and swords.

While some children carefully consider what to do about the central structure, most stay at the edges of the room searching for things: opening up paper recycling bins, dragging stools and chairs in to play along, bringing baskets, buckets, papier-mâché bowls, and bits of string. An orchestra-parade emerges: Children march around the room and encircle the tower to the rhythm of paper tubes hitting the ground. Otis cautiously touches the tower with his tube and then joins a group of children playing hockey with theirs at the end of the room. The tower plays along as a central figure, but over the entire morning it is modified only in shape. The blocks endure.

Time as Lived

It was immediately apparent to all of us that blocks possessed the particular stability of clock time, and that their movements were structured. We noticed that the rhythms of doing and undoing—not just undoing the block structures, but loosening the weight of expectations—which were present with other materials were absent in the block play. The doings with other materials always encompassed finding ways to keep things in motion. We decided to wait. And waiting long enough (that is, following the flows of life as opposed to clock time) helped us work with the unpredictability of life itself. It was an accident that destroyed the blocks' structured time.

> *Otis circumnavigates the room with a long paper tube still in hand. He moves between groups of children who are working together on different arrangements and structures. Walking past one group, he lightly taps their block structure with his tube, just one tap, and then moves on to the next structure. Tap. Tap, tap, tap. These initial light taps have little effect. Then swiftly, with one sharp swing, Otis hits the tall central tower and it falls apart. Other children turn to look, their shock quickly turning to delight as they swoop in to grab loose blocks. Otis moves toward the next structure, his steps deliberate and intentional. Pausing momentarily to stare intently, in one strike he topples these blocks too. He stands for a while, watching the undone piles, and then advances to another structure.*
>
> *Otis's transgressive action is magical in its effects: the blocks are no longer "used up." We could imagine him as a magician with a magic wand: One strike and the spell is broken. The blocks are free and available now for other uses.*

As we watched these events unfold, we wondered about the undoing of structures, how accidents (intended and unintended) are essential in keeping things in motion. The physicist Karen Barad (2007) tells us there is no "external parameter called time," nor "a container called space" (p. 179). Elizabeth Grosz (1999a, 1999b, 2005a, 2005b) makes a similar argument. Following the writings of Deleuze and Bergson, Grosz questions the epistemic, ontological, and political status of time. Time, she states, is not a neutral medium in which life can be framed or matter constructed. Rather, time is an active and dynamic component in the actual framing of life. Grosz's (1999a) interest is specifically in the opening "of time to futurity" (p. 3). Time, for her, becomes a materializing force "whose movements and operations have an inherent element of surprise, unpredictability, or newness" (p. 4). And for Barad (2007), time (or, more precisely, temporality) is "produced and iteratively reconfigured in the materialization of phenomena and the (re)making of material-discursive boundaries and their constitutive exclusions" (p. 179). Space, time, and matter

> are intra-actively produced in the ongoing differential articulation of the world. Time is not a succession of evenly spaced intervals available as a referent to all bodies and space is not a collection of preexisting points set out as a container for matter to inhabit.
>
> *(Barad, 2007, p. 234)*

What might it mean to think about time as an intensive flow? How might we, as Grosz (1999b) writes, notice "the particularity of the duration of events and processes" (p. 18)? How might we pay attention to what endures, to how moments stay with us? And, more importantly, how could we work with the possibilities these enduring experiences, these intensities, might bring?

Time as Intensity

We continued to disrupt the stability of the blocks. What if we took them outside and connected them to more organic, free-flowing forms? Brian Massumi (2002) explains that intensity seems to be "associated with nonlinear processes: resonation and feedback that momentarily suspend the linear progress of the narrative present from past to future" (p. 26). Intensity involves suspense and disruption. "It is like a temporal sink," Massumi says, "a hole in time. . . . It is not exactly passivity because it is filled with motion, resonation. And yet it is not yet activity" (p. 26).

In our block events, the early childhood education objectives for blocks disappeared. Blocks were not blocks anymore. They attracted other materials, perhaps even *needed* other materials to help them resist the weight of expectation/history/clock-time, to help them stay alive.

We place small arrangements of blocks on the outdoor stairway and the sidewalk leading to the studio door. The blocks follow the line of the pathway to the open door, as if to invite the children inside. We gather stones from the garden, add them to the columns of blocks, and position them in circle and crescent shapes, tucking leaves and blossoms in between.

"Look, they're lined up, just like we are," Sareeta exclaims. (Echoes of regulation in early childhood education. It seems we can never get away from this.) Other children notice more stones lying on the stairs and want to collect them. They search for the "most beautiful ones" they can find to add to the line.

The blocks seem at home outside. Their geometric shapes echo the buildings', while the cement stairway seems to call out to the stones, leaves, and flowers: "Come and play!" The children fill their pockets and bring handfuls of stones inside to join the blocks in the room.

The blocks seemed to need and attract other materials. Over the weeks it fascinated us to see the different things that found their way into the room and stayed. We started with the boxes of blocks: the cardboard boxes, packing paper, and wooden blocks. Soon after, to counter the blocks' rigidity, we brought in a collection of soft woolen hearts that had been knitted and felted. We brought textured driftwood sticks worn smooth by the ocean, small balls of gray plasticine, paper tubes of different sizes and in different stages of coming apart. Gradually the block-event collection grew to encompass papier-mâché blocks, stones, a few flowers, yellow/blue binoculars, a small yellow plastic bucket, several baskets, one small plastic container, reams of wax paper taken from the paper recycling bin or borrowed from the paper explorations in the studio, small squares of white paper, other small blocks, cut-up tree branches brought by the children from the studio and the children's center, clipboards, pencils, children's and adults' chairs, several small papier-mâché bowls, bus tickets, coconut shells, two mini Polaroid photos, a paper crown, and a black witch's hat.

In this entanglement of materials, an unexplainable intensity takes place. This intensity compels us to engage with temporalities in early childhood education in different ways. As we worked with the possibilities of this intensity, *duration* emerged.

The concept of duration helps us to understand time as particular to bodily experiences (Bergson, 1991). Perhaps time is an external state that organizes a body's movements. Perhaps it is not discrete compartments that follow one another but an internal, unified, multiple flow of difference. Dynamic.

How does time endure in bodies? How do different bodies experience it differently? When we see time as becoming, as duration, we can see that it doesn't exist as an organizational structure outside of, or regardless of, bodies. As duration, time is particular to a body's experience of it. Coleman (2008) writes:

> Enduring things . . . are the ways in which certain things transform and become, that is move from "the past" and are re-experienced and assembled as different, novel, intensive, temporalities. Enduring things are . . . what a body *is* living (through) as non-linear durations.
>
> *(p. 93, emphasis in original)*

> The past is . . . to be re-experienced through its intensity, through the endurance of a past thing, its connection with the present and future. . . . Moments of intense experience are not self-contained or bounded units (extensity). Rather, the jump or leap involved in remembering and re-experiencing a past moment is a connection between different durations where these durations are assembled simultaneously.
>
> *(p. 94)*

Blocks provoked us to engage with everything each moment entails.

Two boys sit on chairs arranged as a bus. Three chairs, one behind another in a row. The driver leans back, relaxing in his chair, hands extended as if he is driving, a small Polaroid photo in his hand. The passenger loads armfuls of long paper tubes onto an empty chair behind the driver. The pace is relaxed as they chat

> *together and drive nowhere in particular. They observe the block building that is taking place all around them, occasionally stopping to exchange a small chair for a larger one, slowly enlarging the space of the bus as more chairs are added. Another child, with yellow binoculars around her neck, joins in, keeping pace, contributing to the paper-tube pile. You can see her momentary hesitation as she stands on the outskirts of the bus game, briefly apprehends the situation, and moves in. Much like a rope-skipping game, she seems to feel the rhythm of what is happening before she enters the game. Slowly the bus expands, other bodies join, long sticks join the tubes, baskets of blocks are piled on empty chairs, small paper bowls are added as food. The idea of the bus slowly grows. This bus doesn't seem to be moving forward as if heading to a destination. Instead, it is expanding outward, getting fuller, moving with rhythms of gathering, of pausing to look at what's been gathered.*

Artist Leah Oates's (n.d.) work speaks of intense moments as transitory. More than simple spaces in time that we move through, she says, they are complex. Much exists in them. They are messy and unpredictable. They don't leave things behind; they look into the future; they are the past. They include hundreds of small gestures, motions acted out, sounds heard, words spoken, images recorded, the wonder, the many confusions, the intensity of the whole moment. Oates's art makes visible the overlooked, the things we are missing when we talk about a moment as a discrete chunk of time.

All the messiness and complexities that these transitory spaces bring with them are full of potential.

Transitory Spaces

> *"We have to go in about five minutes, children. Five minutes, okay?" The children at first don't pay much attention to their teacher's five-minute warning. They are still gathering in ideas. A few sticks are picked up, wrapped in wax paper, and passed from one child to another, but the bundles open and the sticks spill out. Tubes are picked up from their configuration on the chair, and the pile falls apart. Feet brush against the fallen tubes, spreading them out. The noise intensifies.*
>
> *"One minute," Kelsey says. "We have to go in one minute." Suddenly everything comes undone and everyone springs into action. Sticks and tubes are pulled out of baskets and tubs, wax paper is shaken out, bodies slip and slide, feet knock against chairs and tubes, buckets are dumped out. Shannon, her body in constant motion since the one-minute warning, picks up a cylindrical block and a coconut*

shell. As others begin to line up at the door, she climbs onto a stool in the middle of the room. Knocking the two hard objects together, she seems to measure out every last bit of time, the rhythmic click-click filling every last moment. Finally, the children leave the room and she runs to join them.

Thinking about transitory spaces, rather than transitions, might mean becoming immersed in "intensive" moments, becoming open to what these moments might bring. Brian Massumi (2002) speaks about navigating such moments:

> In every situation there are any number of levels of organization and tendencies in play, in cooperation with each other or at cross-purposes. The way all the elements interrelate is so complex that it isn't necessarily comprehensible in one go. There's always a sort of vagueness surrounding the situation, an uncertainty about where you might be able to go and what you might be able to do once you exit that particular context. This uncertainty can actually be empowering—once you realise that it gives you a margin of maneuverability and you focus on that, rather than on projecting success or failure. It gives you the feeling that there is always an opening to experiment, to try and see. This brings a sense of potential to the situation.
>
> (p. xx)

We become experimenters with time.

We notice a pattern: At the end of the morning when the five-minute warning is given, everything speeds up. The closer we get to being "out of time," the more inventive the children become. The moments between staying and leaving are incredibly dynamic and highly charged. As soon as an educator mentions that only one or two minutes are left, the rhythm of play takes on new energy and intensity. There are constant, rapid improvisations as one thing becomes another and storylines intersect. Block structures fall down; children run; hands suddenly, urgently, need to touch everything; feet need to jump over blocks; every last bit of time needs to be savored. All the "block rules" are freely broken.

The transition itself is more than the now. It is filled with intensities and affects, and these intensities and affects become a multitude of potentialities.

One morning after the one-minute warning, Shannon looks at Kelsey and asks, "Is this a big minute or a small minute?"

We begin to understand time as felt, as a bodied sense of expansiveness or constriction.

AFTERWORD

Noticing

Every encounter with materials involves decisions about what, and in what way, to notice. Using a camera means you have to look somewhere. The challenge in photographing and in some way recording children's experimentations is that it is often difficult to know or to recognize what is really happening. Where should I look? At what should I look? How should I look?

What is important to us about paper or charcoal or paint or clay or blocks, and what we already understand about a material, process, or situation, may not be what concerns children, and, in particular, may not concern these children here at this time and in this place. Even more puzzling is how to see and enter the between-space, the space of intra-active (Lenz Taguchi, 2010), event-full entanglements where children, materials, spaces, places, educators, time move together, where children and educators are there but not always in charge of what goes on, and where something we can't fully comprehend is happening.

In this project we have tried to pay attention to the incomprehensible: gesture, movement, a glance or look, a pause, moments of hesitation, times of gathering, collecting, and dispersal; acts of doing and undoing. We have been interested in the play between bodies, our participation and implication in the midst of everything, and what Anna Tsing (2013) calls the serious work of noticing. This book was an opportunity to pause and consider these acts of paying attention, to consider what noticing does and what is produced by noticing. We are convinced that something is always produced in these acts of attentiveness.

We attended to materials' fluxes and flows (Ingold, 2011) and to times of intensity and pause, moments of confusion and undoing. Our paying attention led us to attend to coverings and uncoverings, makings and remakings, comings and goings. To the rhythms of repetition—rhythms that, although seemingly inconsequential, produced many small, yet vibrant, variances. It led us to the motions of again and again and again and again, to the verbs and doings (Ingold, 2013), to how things are their movements and stories.

As we paid attention to all these things, it brought them more clearly into view, which in turn amplified what was already going on. It encouraged us to give more space to the material so the material had more play. We attended to how paper slipped under the door and blanketed the hallway floor after every studio event. We noticed its delightful airy waywardness, its desire to take flight, which, as a result, brought paper to meet fan, wind, and the large outdoor vent. We noticed how charcoal spreads, moves, covers, and infiltrates the places it enters, and so sought to design spaces where the charcoal could move freely. Paying attention invited us to work more playfully and also much more seriously with the materials.

Noticing materials' movements and ways generated a great deal of expectancy, not just in children's creativity and innovativeness, but in the play of the material, in the spaces between, and in everyone's anticipation of what might emerge. What would clay do next? Where might blocks lead us? We felt surprise, delight, frustration, puzzlement, and, at times, genuine bewilderment. Most of what we experienced together with the children exceeded our capacity to know, but knowing was never our aim. We were less concerned with understanding what was going on than we were with paying close attention to the fluxes, movements, and rhythms of the materials, the indefinite and unpredictable encounters, and the generative forces and relations among, with, and between children and materials.

We think we can say that, as a result of this project, we are learning to see differently.

In the project and the book, we have been interested in doing more than reporting on experience, relaying information, or describing the world as we think it is. Our goal has not been to capture or accurately record, even if we could, the divergent and inventive processes of children; the many transitory, ephemeral, and inconclusive acts; or the movements and lives of materials. Rather, being aware that methods produce realities (Law, 2004), we set out to open our perception to the vibrant entanglements, assemblages, ecologies, and intra-actions, to speculate about how the world might be, so that we could carefully, ethically, and attentively respond to, and enter more fully into, children's movements and encounters and the vibrant life of things.

REFERENCES

Ainsworth, M. D. (1969). Object relations, dependency and attachment: A theoretical review of the infant–mother relationship. *Child Development, 40*, 967–1025.

Anderson, B., Kearnes, M., McFarlane, C., & Swanton, D. (2012). On assemblages and geography. *Dialogues in Human Geography, 2*(2), 171–189. doi: 10.1177/2043820612449261

Atkinson, D. (2011). *Art, equality, and learning: Pedagogies against the state.* Rotterdam, The Netherlands: Sense.

Barad, K. (2007). *Meeting the universe halfway: Quantum physics and the entanglement of matter and meaning.* Durham, NC: Duke University Press.

Barad, K. (2011). Posthumanist performativity: Toward an understanding of how matter comes to matter. *Signs, 28*(3), 801–831. Retrieved from: http://www.jstor.org/stable/10.1086/345321

Bennett, J. (2004). The force of things: Steps toward an ecology of matter. *Political Theory, 32*(3), 347–372. Retrieved from: http://www.jstor.org/stable/4148158

Bennett, J. (2010). *Vibrant matter: A political ecology of things.* Durham, NC: Duke University Press.

Benso, S. (2000). *The face of things: A different side of ethics.* Albany, NY: SUNY Press.

Bergson, H. (1991). *Creative evolution.* Mineola, NY: Dover.

Boorstin, D. J. (1983). *The discoverers.* New York, NY: Random House.

Bowlby, J. (1969). *Attachment and loss.* Vol. 1. Attachment. New York, NY: Basic Books.

Bowlby, J. (1973). *Attachment and loss.* Vol. 2. Separation. New York, NY: Basic Books.

Bowlby, J. (1980). *Attachment and loss.* Vol. 3. Loss. New York, NY: Basic Books.

Bronfenbrenner, U. (1979). *The ecology of human development.* Cambridge, MA: Harvard University Press.

Callaghan, K. (2002). Nurturing the enthusiasm and ideals of new teachers through reflective practice. *Canadian Children, 27*(1), 38–41.

Canatella, H. (2006). Is beauty an archaic spirit in education? *Journal of Aesthetic Education, 40*(1), 94–103.

Carey, J. (1989). *Communication as culture: Essays on media and society.* New York, NY: Unwin Hyman.

Carter, M., & Curtis, D. (2007). *Learning together with young children: A curriculum framework for reflective teachers.* St. Paul, MN: Redleaf.

Casarino, C. (2003). Time matters: Marx, Negri, Agamben and the corporeal. *Strategies, 16*(2), 185–206.

Ceppi, G., & Zini, M. (Eds.). (2008). *Children, space, relations: Metaproject for an environment for young children.* Reggio Emilia, Italy: Reggio Children and Domus Academy.

Clark, A. (2005). Ways of seeing: Using the Mosaic approach to listen to young children's perspectives. In A. Clark, A. Trine Kjorhot, & P. Moss (Eds.), *Beyond listening: Children's perspectives on early childhood services* (pp. 29–49). Bristol, England: The Policy Press.

Close, H. (2007). The use of photography as a qualitative research tool. *Nurse Researcher, 15*(1), 27–36.

Colebrook, C. (2002). *Gilles Deleuze.* London, England: Routledge.

Coleman, R. (2008). Things that stay: Feminist theory, duration and the future. *Time & Society, 17*(1), 85–102.

Coleman, R. (2009). *The becoming of bodies: Girls, images, experience.* Manchester, England: Manchester University Press.

Csikszentmihalyi, M. (1990). *Flow: The psychology of optimal experience.* New York, NY: Harper & Row.

Dahlberg, G., & Moss, P. (2005). *Ethics and politics in early childhood education.* London, England: RoutledgeFalmer.

Dahlberg, G., & Moss, P. (2009). Foreword. In L. Olssen (Ed.), *Movement and experimentation in young children's learning: Deleuze and Guattari in early childhood education* (pp. xiii–xxviii). New York, NY: Routledge.

Davies, B. (2014). *Listening to children: Being and becoming.* New York, NY: Routledge.

Deleuze, G. (1997). *Desire and pleasure* (Trans. M. McMahon). Retrieved from: http://www.artdes.monash.edu.au/globe/delfou.html

Deleuze, G. (2006). *Bergsonism* (6th ed.). New York, NY: Zone Books.

Deleuze, G., & Guattari, F. (1987). *A thousand plateaus: Capitalism and schizophrenia.* Minneapolis, MN: University of Minnesota Press.

Dewey, J. (1897, January). My pedagogic creed. *School Journal, 54,* 77–80. Retrieved from: http://dewey.pragmatism.org/creed.htm

Dewey, J. (1916). Democracy and education. New York, NY: Free Press.

Dittmer, J. (2013/2014). Geopolitical assemblages and complexity. *Progress in Human Geography, 38*(3), 385–401. Retrieved from: http://phg.sagepub.com/content/38/3/385.full

Foucault, M. (1977). *Discipline and punish: The birth of the prison.* New York, NY: Vintage.

Fraser, S. (2006). *Authentic childhood: Experiencing Reggio Emilia in the classroom.* Toronto, ON: Nelson.

Friends of Reggio. (2004). *Remida day.* Reggio Emilia, Italy: Reggio Children s.r.l.

Gerst, B. (1998). Further reflections on the application of the Reggio view in a kindergarten classroom. *Canadian Children, 23*(2), 43–48.

Gerst, B. (2002). Making kindergarten meaningful: The bird study. *Canadian Children, 27*(2), 12–16.

Gerst, B. (2003). Exploring an essential question: How can bears and humans share our earth peacefully? *Canadian Children, 28*(2), 36–43.

Gilbert, J. (2004). Becoming-music: The rhizomatic moment of improvisation. In I. Buchanan & M. Swiboda (Eds.), *Deleuze and music* (pp. 118–139). Edinburgh, Scotland: University of Edinburgh Press.

Goldsworthy, A. (n.d.). *In his own words.* Retrieved from: http://www.morning-earth.org/ARTISTNATURALISTS/AN_Goldsworthy.html

Golomb, C. (1992). *The child's creation of a pictorial world.* Berkeley, CA: University of California Press.

Greene, M. (1984). The art of being present: Educating for aesthetic encounters. *Journal of Education, 166*(2), 123–135.

Grosz, E. (1999a). Becoming: An introduction. In E. Grosz (Ed.), *Becomings: Explorations in time, memory, and futures* (pp. 1–12). New York, NY: Cornell University Press.

Grosz, E. (1999b). Thinking the new: Of futures yet unthought. In E. Grosz (Ed.), *Becomings: Explorations in time, memory, and futures* (pp. 15–28). New York, NY: Cornell University Press.

Grosz, E. (2005a). *Time travels: Feminism, nature, power.* Durham, NC: Duke University Press.

Grosz, E. (2005b). *The nick of time: Politics, evolution and the untimely.* Durham, NC: Duke University Press.

Guattari, F. (1995). *Chaosmosis: An ethico-aesthetic paradigm.* Bloomington, IN: Indiana University Press.

Haraway, D. (1988). Situated knowledges: The science question in feminism and the privilege of partial perspective. *Feminist Studies, 14*(3), 575–599.

Haraway, D. (2008). *When species meet.* Minneapolis, MN: University of Minnesota Press.

Haraway, D. (2015, June 30). Anthropocene, Capitalocene, Chthulucene: Staying with the trouble. *Anthropocene: Arts of living on a damaged planet.* Open Transcripts. Retrieved from: http://opentranscripts.org/transcript/anthropocene-capitalocene-chthulucene/

Hodgins, D. (2014). *(Re)Storying dolls and cars: Gender and care with young children.* Master's thesis, University of Victoria, British Columbia, Canada. Retrieved from: https://dspace.library.uvic.ca/handle/1828/5740

Honegger, D. S. (n.d.). *Journey into early childhood: Construction/block play.* Retrieved from: http://journeyintoearlychildhood.weebly.com/the-importance-of-block-play.html

Ingold, T. (2011). *Being alive: Essays on movement, knowledge, and description.* New York, NY: Routledge.

Ingold, T. (2013). *Making: Anthropology, archeology, art, and architecture* (Kindle version). New York, NY: Routledge.

Kimmerer, R. W. (2003). *Gathering moss: A natural and cultural history of mosses.* Corvallis, OR: OSU Press.

Kind, S. (2007). In open spaces. In L. F. Darling, A. Clarke, & G. Erickson (Eds.), *Collective improvisation in a teacher education community* (pp. 67–74). Dordrecht, The Netherlands: Springer.

Kind, S., & Pacini-Ketchabaw, V. (2016). Charcoal intensities and risky experimentations. In H. Skott-Myhre, V. Pacini-Ketchabaw, & K. Skott-Myhre (Eds.), *Youth work, early education, and psychology: Liminal encounters* (pp. 93–111). Critical Cultural Studies of Early Childhood series. New York, NY: Springer.

Kocher, L. (1999). The rabbit habitat: Documenting a kindergarten project. *Canadian Children, 24*(2), 15–22.

Kocher, L. (2004). The disposition to document: Portraits of practice. *Canadian Children, 29*(1), 23–31.

Kocher, L. (2009). Setting our little sails: Pedagogical documentation as a phenomenological act. In L. Iannicci & P. Whitty (Eds.), *Early childhood curricula: Reconceptualist perspectives* (pp. 121–140). Calgary, AB: Destelig.

Kocher, L. (2010). Families and pedagogical narration: Disrupting traditional understandings of family involvement. In V. Pacini-Ketchabaw (Ed.), *Flows, rhythms, and intensities of early childhood education* (pp. 177–201). New York, NY: Peter Lang.

Koepke, M. (2015). Towards a pedagogy of moments: Radical pedagogies. *Inflexions, 8*. Retrieved from: http://www.inflexions.org/radicalpedagogy/main.html#Koepke

Kummen, K. (2010). Is it time to put 'tidy up time' away? Contesting routines and transitions in early childhood spaces. In V. Pacini-Ketchabaw (Ed.), *Flows, rhythms, and intensities of early childhood education curriculum* (pp. 97–112). New York, NY: Peter Lang.

Latour, B. (2005a). *Reassembling the social: An introduction to actor-network theory.* Oxford, England: Oxford University Press.

Latour, B. (2005b). What is given in experience? A review of Isabelle Stengers 'Pensée avec Whitehead'. *Boundary 2, 32*(1), 222–237. Retrieved from: http://www.bruno-latour.fr/sites/default/files/93-STENGERS-GB.pdf

Law, J. (2004). *After method: Mess in social science research.* New York, NY: Routledge.

Lehrer, J. (2012). *Imagine: How creativity works.* Toronto, ON: Penguin.

Lenz Taguchi, H. (2010). *Going beyond the theory/practice divide in early childhood education: Introducing an intra-active pedagogy.* New York, NY: Routledge.

Levine, R. (1998). *A geography of time: The temporal misadventures of a social psychologist, or how every culture keeps time just a little bit differently.* New York, NY: Basic Books.

Lowenfeld, V., & Brittain, W. L. (1987). *Creative and mental growth* (8th ed.). New York, NY: Macmillan.

MacDonald-Carlson, H. (1997). The story of the room. *Canadian Children, 22*(1), 34–37.

MacDonald-Carlson, H. (2003). Developing a sense of place: Exploring ideas of home and community. *Canadian Children, 28*(2), 10–16.

Manning, E. (2007). *Politics of touch: Sense, movement, sovereignty.* Minneapolis, MN: University of Minnesota Press.

Manning, E. (2009). Taking the next step: Touch as technique. *Senses and Society, 4*(2), 211–226.

Manning, E. (2010). Always more than one: The collectivity of a life. *Body & Society, 16*(1), 117–127. doi: 10.1177/1357034X09354128

Manning, E., & Massumi, B. (2014). *Thought in the act: Passages in the ecology of experience.* Minneapolis, MN: University of Minnesota Press.

Massumi, B. (1987). Introduction. In G. Deleuze & F. Guattari (Eds.), *A thousand plateaus: Capitalism and schizophrenia* (pp. ix–xv). Minneapolis, MN: University of Minnesota Press.

Massumi, B. (2002). *Parables for the virtual: Movement, affect, sensation.* Durham, NC: Duke University Press.

Matthews, J. (2003). *Drawing and painting: Children and visual representation* (2nd ed.). Thousand Oaks, CA: SAGE.

McNiff, S. (2008). Art-based research. In J. G. Knowles & A. L. Cole (Eds.), *Handbook of the arts in qualitative research* (pp. 29–40). Thousand Oaks, CA: SAGE.

Navab, A. (2001). Re-picturing photography: A language in the making. *Journal of Aesthetic Education, 35*(1), 69–84.

Oates, L. (n.d.). *Artist's statement.* Retrieved from: http://leahoates.com/

O'Donoghue, D. (2015). The turn to experience in contemporary art: A potentiality for thinking art education differently. *Studies in Art Education, 56*(2), 103–113.

Olssen, L. (2009). *Movement and experimentation in young children's learning: Deleuze and Guattari in early childhood education.* New York, NY: Routledge.

O'Sullivan, S. (2006). *Art encounters Deleuze and Guattari: Thought beyond representation.* London, England: Palgrave Macmillan.

Pacini-Ketchabaw, V. (Ed.). (2010). *Flows, rhythms, and intensities of early childhood education.* New York, NY: Peter Lang.

Pacini-Ketchabaw, V. (2012). Acting with the clock: Clocking practices in early childhood. *Contemporary Issues in Early Childhood, 13*(2), 154–160.

Pacini-Ketchabaw, V. (2013). Politicizing transitions in early childhood. *Global Studies of Childhood, 3*(3), 221–229.

Pelo, A. (2007). *The language of art: Inquiry-based studio practices in early childhood settings.* St. Paul, MN: Redleaf.

Peters, G. (2009). *The philosophy of improvisation.* Chicago, IL: University of Chicago Press.

Prochner, L. (2011). 'Their little wooden bricks': A history of the material culture of kindergarten in the United States. *Paedagogica Historica, 47*(3), 355–375. doi: 10.1080/00309230.2010.513688

Puig de la Bellacasa, M. (2015). Making time for soil: Technoscientific futurity and the pace of care. *Social Studies of Science, 45*(5), 691–716. doi: 10.1177/0306312715599851

Rautio, P. (2013). Being nature: Interspecies articulation as a species-specific practice of relating to environment. *Environmental Education Research, 19*(4), 445–457.

Richards, R. D. (2009). Young visual ethnographers: Children's use of photography to record, share and extend their art experiences. *International Art in Early Childhood Research Journal, 1*(1), 1–16. Retrieved from: http://artinearlychildhood.org/artec/images/article/ARTEC_2009_Research_Journal_1_Article_3.pdf

Richmond, S. (2004). Remembering beauty: Reflections of Kant and Cartier-Bresson for aspiring photographers. *Journal of Aesthetic Education, 38*(1), 78–88.

Rose, D. B. (2004). *Reports from a wild country: Ethics for decolonisation.* Sydney, AU: University of New South Wales.

Rose, S., & Whitty, P. (2010). Where do we find the time to do this? Struggling against the tyranny of time. *Alberta Journal of Educational Research, 56*(3), 257–273.

Rosen, R. (2009). Examining early childhood spaces: Creating Sunland. *Canadian Children, 34*(2), 38–41.

Rule, A., & Stewart, R. (2002). Effects of practical life materials on kindergarteners' fine motor skills. *Early Childhood Education Journal, 30*(1), 9–13.

Sawhney, H. (2004). The slide towards decentralization: Clock and computer. *Media, Culture & Society, 26*(3), 359–374. doi: 10.1177/0163443704042257

Scarry, E. (1999). *On beauty and being just.* Princeton, NJ: Princeton University Press.

Sontag, S. (1977). *On photography.* New York, NY: Farrar, Straus, & Giroux.

Springgay, S. (2011). The ethico-aesthetics of affect and a sensational pedagogy. *Journal of the Canadian Association for Curriculum Studies, 9*(1), 66–82.

Springgay, S. (2012). Tasting the m/other as sensational pedagogy. In S. Springgay & D. Freedman (Eds.), *Mothering a bodied curriculum: Emplacement, desire, affect* (pp. 255–269). Toronto, ON: University of Toronto Press.

Springgay, S., & Rotas, N. (2014). How do you make a classroom operate like a work of art? Deleuzeguattarian methodologies of research-creation. *International Journal of Qualitative Studies in Education, 25*(5), 552–572. doi: 10.1080/09518398.2014.933913

Stengers, I. (2005). An ecology of practices. *Cultural Studies Review, 11*(1), 183–196.

Stengers, I. (2007, September 2). Gilles Deleuze's last message. *Recalcitrance*. Retrieved from: http://www.recalcitrance.com/deleuzelast.htm

Stengers, I. (2008a). A constructivist reading of process and reality. *Theory, Culture, & Society, 25*(4), 91–110. doi: 10.1177/0263276408091985

Stengers, I. (2008b). Experimenting with refrains: Subjectivity and the challenge of escaping modern dualism. *Subjectivity, 22*, 38–59. doi: 10.1057/sub.2008.6

Stengers, I. (2015). *In catastrophic times: Resisting the coming barbarism* (A. Goffey, Trans.). Open Humanities Press & Meson Press. Retrieved from: http://meson.press/wp-content/uploads/2015/11/978-1-78542-010-8_In-Catastrophic-Times_Stengers.pdf

Stengers, I., Manning, E., & Massumi, B. (2009). History through the middle: Between macro and mesopolitics. *Inflexions, 3*. Retrieved from: http://www.inflexions.org/n3_History-through-the-Middle-Between-Macro-and-Mesopolitics-1.pdf

Sturken, M., & Cartwright, L. (2009). *Practices of looking*. New York, NY: Oxford University Press.

Tarr, P. (2005). Drawing at the centre. *Canadian Children, 30*(1), 4–8.

Tarr, P., Bjartveit, C., Kostiuk, L., & McCowan, D. (2009). Supporting imagination in play through pedagogical documentation: Haunted houses, fairies and goblins, pirates and islands. *Canadian Children, 34*(1), 21–28.

Taylor, A., & Pacini-Ketchabaw, V. (2015). Learning with children, ants, and worms in the Anthropocene: Towards a common world pedagogy of multispecies vulnerability. *Pedagogy, Culture, and Society, 23*(4), 507–529. doi: 10.1080/14681366.2015.1039050

Thiele, K. (2014). *Ethos* of diffraction: New paradigms for a (post)humanist ethics. *Parallax, 20*(3), 202–216.

Thompson, C. M. (2008). Action, autobiography, and aesthetics in young children's self-initiated drawings. *Journal of Art and Design Education, 18*(2), 155–161. doi: 10.1111/1468-5949.00169

Toumayayan, A. P. (2004). *Encountering the other: The artwork and the problem of difference in Blanchot and Levinas*. Pittsburg, PA: Duquesne University Press.

Trimis, E., & Savva, A. (2009). Artistic learning in relation to young children's chorotopos: An in-depth approach to early childhood visual culture education. *Early Childhood Education Journal, 36*, 527–539.

Tsing, A. (2005). *Friction: An ethnography of global connection*. Princeton, NJ: Princeton University Press.

Tsing, A. (2011, May). Arts of inclusion, or, how to love a mushroom. *Australian Humanities Review, 50*. Retrieved from: http://www.australianhumanitiesreview.org/archive/Issue-May-2011/tsing.html

Tsing, A. (2012). On nonscalability: The living world is not amenable to precision-nested scales. *Common Knowledge, 18*(3), 505–524. doi: 10.1215/0961754X-1630424

Tsing, A. (2013). More than human sociality: A call for critical description. In K. Hastrup (Ed.), *Anthropology and nature* (pp. 27–42). New York, NY: Routledge.

van Dooren, T. (2014). *Flight ways: Life and loss at the edge of extinction*. New York, NY: Columbia University Press.

van Dooren, T., & Rose, D. B. (forthcoming). *Encountering a more-than-human world: Ethos and the arts of witness*. [abstract]. Retrieved from: http://thomvandooren.org/papers-in-progress/

Vecchi, V. (2010). *Art and creativity in Reggio Emilia: Exploring the role and potentials of ateliers in early childhood education*. New York, NY: Routledge.

Vecchi, V., & Giudici, C. (Eds.). (2004). *Children, art, artists: The expressive languages of children, the artistic language of Alberto Burri*. Reggio Emilia, Italy: Reggio Children s.r.l.

Wien, C. A. (1996). Time, work, and developmentally appropriate practice. *Early Childhood Research Quarterly, 11*, 377–403.

Wien, C. A. (2008). *Emergent curriculum in the primary classroom: Interpreting the Reggio Emilia approach in schools.* New York, NY: Teachers College Press.

Wien, C. A., & Kirby-Smith, S. (1998). Untiming the curriculum: A case study of removing clocks from the program. *Young Children, 53*(5), 8–13.

Winston, J. (2008). *Beauty and education.* New York, NY: Routledge.

Wolseley, J. (2009/2010). *A natural history of swamps II, purple swamphen—Gwydir wetlands.* Retrieved from: http://johnwolseley.net/exhibitions/carboniferous

Wolseley, J. (2016). *Artist website.* Retrieved from: http://johnwolseley.net/home

Wong, A. (2006). A whole new world: Documenting in the infant classroom. *Canadian Children, 31*(2), 32–37.

Young, K. (2001). Practicing the ideas of Reggio Emilia: A growing experience. *Canadian Children, 26*(1), 28–32.

Zhang, O. (n.d.). *Horizon statement.* Retrieved from: http://ozhang.com/Site/O_Zhang,_HStatement.html

Zhang, O. (2009, August 11). *O Zhang talks about her work at Vancouver Art Gallery Offsite.* Retrieved from: https://www.facebook.com/video/video.php?v=135155947512

Zylinska, J. (2014). *Minimal ethics for the Anthropocene.* Ann Arbor, MI: Open Humanities Press. Retrieved from: http://quod.lib.umich.edu/cgi/p/pod/dod-idx/minimal-ethics-for-the-anthropocene.pdf?c=ohp;idno=12917741.0001.001

INDEX